鳥 山　明

ABOUT the CREATOR

Widely known all over the world for his playful, innovative storytelling and humorous, distinctive art style, **Dragon Ball** creator Akira Toriyama is also known in his native Japan for the wildly popular **Dr. Slump**, his previous manga series about the adventures of a mad scientist and his android "daughter." His hit series **Dragon Ball** ran from 1984 to 1995 in Shueisha's weekly **Shônen Jump** magazine. He is also known for his design work on video games such as **Dragon Warrior**, **Chrono Trigger** and **Tobal No. 1**. His recent manga works include **Cowa**, **Kajika**, **Sand Land**, and the short self-parody **Neko Majin Z**. He lives with his family in Tokyo, Japan.

DRAGON BALL Z VOL. 5

This graphic novel contains the monthly comic series DRAGON BALL Z PART 3 #1 through #6 in their entirety.

STORY AND ART BY
AKIRA TORIYAMA

ENGLISH ADAPTATION BY
GERARD JONES

Translation/Lillian Olsen
Touch-Up Art & Lettering/Wayne Truman
Cover Design/Hidemi Sahara
Graphics & Layout/Sean Lee
Edited by/Trish Ledoux & Jason Thompson
Collected Edition Edited by/Jason Thompson

Senior Editor/Trish Ledoux
Managing Editor/Hyoe Narita
Editor-in-Chief/Satoru Fujii
Publisher/Seiji Horibuchi
Director of Sales & Marketing/Dallas Middaugh
Marketing Manager/Renée Solberg
Sales Associate/Mike Roberson

© 1984 by BIRD STUDIO. All rights reserved. First Published in Japan in 1984 by SHUEISHA Inc., Tokyo. English translation rights in the United States of America and Canada arranged by SHUEISHA Inc. through CLOVERWAY, INC. No unauthorized reproduction allowed. The stories, characters, and incidents mentioned in this publication are entirely fictional.

New and adapted artwork and text ©2001 Viz Communications, Inc. All rights reserved.

Printed in Canada

Published by Viz Communications, Inc.
P.O. Box 77010 • San Francisco, CA 94107

10 9 8 7 6 5 4 3 2 1
First printing, July 2001

Vizit us at our World Wide Web site at
www.vizkids.com!

VIZ GRAPHIC NOVEL

DRAGON BALL Z

Vol. 5

DB: 21 of 42

STORY AND ART BY

AKIRA TORIYAMA

THE MAIN CHARACTERS

Bulma

Goku's oldest friend, Bulma is a scientific genius. She met Goku while on a quest for the seven magical Dragon Balls which, when gathered together, can grant any wish.

Son Goku

The greatest martial artist on Earth, he owes his strength to the training of Kame-Sen'nin and Kaiô-sama, and the fact that he's one of the alien Saiyans. Has he finally hit his limit?

Kaiô-sama

Also known as the "Lord of Worlds", he is one of the deities of the Dragon Ball universe. He lives in the Other World at the end of the Serpent Road.

Bulma
Kaiôsama
Son Goku
Son Gohan
Kuririn

Kuririn

Goku's former martial arts schoolmate.

Son Gohan

Goku's four-year-old son, a half-human, half-Saiyan with hidden reserves of strength. He was trained by Goku's former enemy Piccolo.

Vegeta
Yajirobe
Kame Sen'nin

Yajirobe

A rough-talking, solitary swordsman, never seen without his *katana* sword and *yukata* robes. Yajirobe is one of Goku's old friends, but he's not exactly heroic.

Vegeta

The prince of Planet Vegeta, homeworld of the Saiyans. He claims to be the greatest fighter in the universe. He originally came to Earth to find the Dragon Balls and wish for immortality, but he was defeated... for now...

Kame-Sen'nin

Kame-Sen'nin, also known as the "Turtle Hermit" or *Muten-Rôshi* (the "Invincible Old Master"), helped train Goku and Kuririn in the martial arts.

Many years ago, a warlike alien race called the Saiyans sent their young in spaceships to distant worlds, in order to colonize the worlds and kill the inhabitants. One of these young was the baby Son Goku, who overcame his evil heritage and became Earth's greatest hero. Years later, the surviving Saiyans—Vegeta, Nappa, and Goku's brother Raditz—returned to Earth to carry out their original mission of destruction and steal Earth's greatest treasure, the Dragon Balls. Nappa and Raditz, and Goku's friends Yamcha, Tenshinhan, Chaozu and Piccolo died in the assault. After a grueling battle, during which he used the secret techniques taught to him by Kaiô-sama, Goku defeated Vegeta...but now all the survivors lie alongside one another in the rubble, as Vegeta summons his ship to retreat into space...

DRAGON BALL Z 5

IT'S THE CONTENTS!

CONTENTS

Tale 47 Goku's Request 7
Tale 48 The Bittersweet End 22
Tale 49 Destination Namek 36
Tale 50 The Mysterious Spaceship 50
Tale 51 3...2...1...Lift Off! 64
Tale 52 The Return of Vegeta 78
Tale 53 Planet Namek, Cold and Dark 92
Tale 54 The Mysterious Strangers 108
Tale 55 Vegeta's True Power! 122
Tale 56 Goku Returns! Again! 136
Tale 57 Son Goku's Spaceship 150
Tale 58 Namekian Fear 164
Title Page Gallery 179

DRAGON BALL

DBZ : 47

Goku's Request

亀

VOOO---N
192

WHICH WAY ?
A LITTLE MORE... TO THE LEFT...

LEFT. GOT IT.

THAT LIGHT! BENEATH THAT LIGHT!

ARE YOU SURE?! ARE YOU **SURE** GOHAN'S ALIVE?!!
I SAID "PROBABLY" !!!
I TOLD YOU WE SHOULD'VE LEFT HER HOME...

"PROBABLY" ISN'T GOOD ENOUGH!!!
WHAT ELSE CAN I SAY...?!
192

THERE ARE FOUR OF THEM THERE... OR FIVE...
BUT I CAN BARELY FEEL THEIR "CHI"... WHAT'S HAPPENED... ?

I...CANNOT SAY... I DID NOT SEE...
GASP
GASP
BUT THE SAIYAN MUST BE BADLY HURT AS WELL...

VNN--N

WH... WHAT... ?

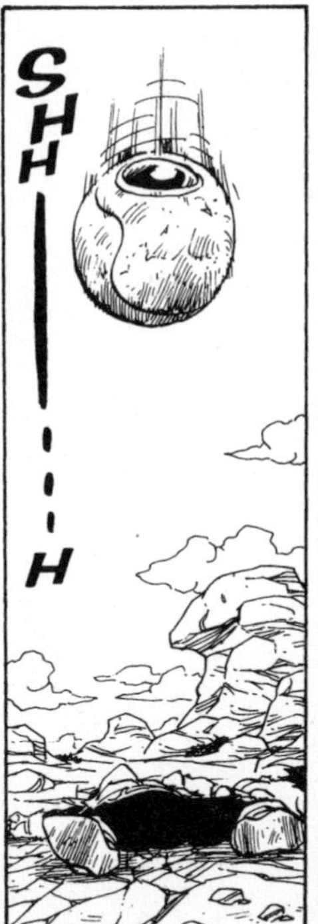
SHH---H

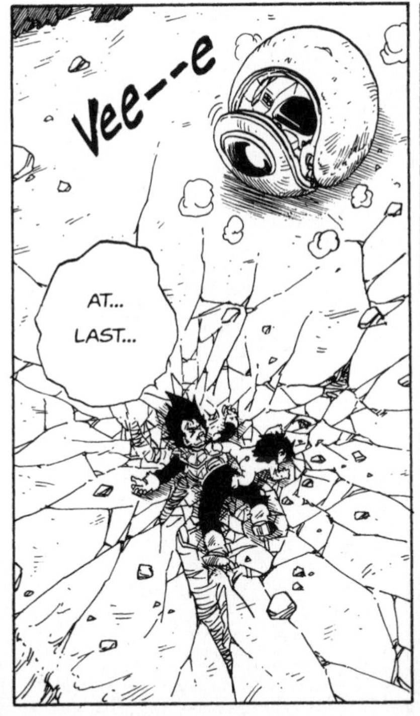
Vee--e
AT... LAST...

N...
NNN...
UH...!!

......

MUH...
MUST
BE...
HIS...
SHIP...
!

SO...
CL...
CLOSE...
D...
DAMN
IT ALL...
WON'T...
LET
HIM...
GET
AWAY...
!!

HUHH
HUHH
SHK...
SHK...

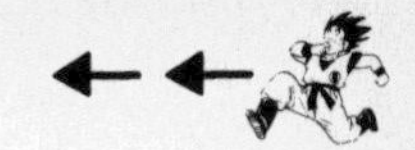

HUF
HUF

WE'VE COME... THIS FAR...
GOTTA... FINISH IT.......

HUF
HUF

OH, MY....THAT WAS CLOSE... YES, YES, CLOSE INDEED....
I SUPPOSE I SHOULDN'T PLAY FAVORITES, BUT THAT SAIYAN HAS BEEN SO MUCH TROUBLE, ALL OVER THE GALAXY....YES, THIS IS BEST.....

...IT'S ONLY TOO BAD THAT THIS WON'T DESTROY THE ROOTS OF EVIL...NO, NO, NOT AT ALL...

...NOT THE ROOTS........

N... NNH...

HFF
HFF
HFF

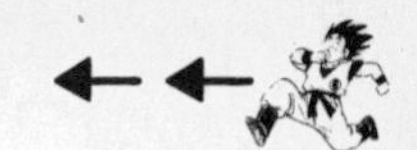

!!
THIS... IS FOR EVERYONE... YOU KILLED... !!

N... NO...... !!!
I CAN'T *MOVE*...... !!

DIE !!!!

KURIRIN, *STOP* !!!!

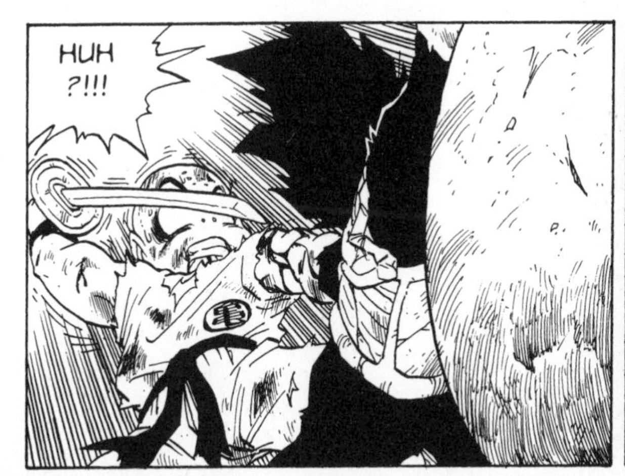
HUH ?!!!

G...
GOKU
?!

!?

W-WAS
THAT...
YOU,
GOKU...
?
TALKIN'
IN
MY
HEAD....
?

I'M TOO
HURT....TO
USE MY
VOICE.....
KURIRIN...
I HAVE
JUST ONE
REQUEST...
PLEASE...
LET THE
SAIYAN
GO....

A-ARE YOU INSANE?! HE KILLED OUR FRIENDS, HE TRIED TO KILL US...
HE TRIED TO KILL EVERYBODY IN THE WHOLE WORLD!

IF WE LET HIM GO NOW, HE'LL REGAIN HIS STRENGTH AND COME BACK AGAIN !!

YEAH... PROBABLY...

ARE YOU THINKING HE'S GONNA SEE THE LIGHT, LIKE PICCOLO? THAT HE'S GONNA TURN OVER A NEW LEAF? WELL, FORGET ABOUT IT!
HE'S NOT LIKE THAT!! HE DOESN'T HAVE A LEAF TO TURN OVER! HE DOESN'T HAVE A SPECK OF DECENCY IN HIM! HE'S A KILLING MACHINE! HE'S A--

I KNOW... AND I KNOW HOW DANGEROUS HE IS...
BUT... I DON'T KNOW HOW TO SAY IT...WHEN I SAW HIM ABOUT TO DIE... I THOUGHT...

WHAT A WASTE...

WHAT A ... "WASTE" ?!

I TRAINED UNDER KAIŌ, THE LORD OF WORLDS... I THOUGHT I'D HIT THE PEAK OF POWER...
BUT VEGETA WAS... SO FAR ABOVE ME...! I WAS SHOCKED... SCARED...

BUT... SOMEWHERE INSIDE...I WAS HAPPY. I WAS... THRILLED... TO BE FIGHTING SUCH POWER...
I GUESS IT'S MY SAIYAN BLOOD... IT'S NOT SMART, I KNOW...

DMP...
...RRR...

BUT NEXT TIME... I SWEAR I'M GONNA SURPASS HIM... GONNA BEAT HIM...!!
I KNOW IT'S WRONG, BUT PLEASE...! LET ME DO IT MYSELF...!!

....
BUT..........

......

TONG...

HFF

YOU SAVED THE EARTH...I GUESS YOU'VE GOT THE RIGHT...TO HAVE IT YOUR WAY...

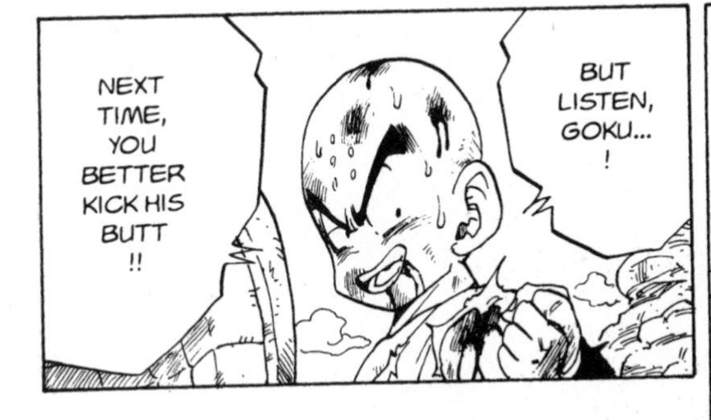
BUT LISTEN, GOKU... !
NEXT TIME, YOU BETTER KICK HIS BUTT !!

HEH!!
YEAH...!

VNN---N

N... NEXT TIME, LITTLE BOYS...
HEHH... THERE WON'T BE... ANY MIRACLES...
H-HAVE FUN...WHILE YOU CAN...

YOU.... STINKING........
T··M

WSS—ISH

T-TMP
T-TMP

IT'S OKAY, GOHAN... IT'S OKAY...

H-HE'S...
...HE'S GONE...?

CAN'T BELIEVE THAT IDIOT...
HE DIDN'T FINISH HIM OFF...?!

SORRY, KURIRIN...
AW, HELL... FORGET ABOUT IT...
WE GOTTA THINK ABOUT THE ONES WHO DIED... SEE IF THERE'S ANY WAY TO BRING 'EM BACK TO...

VOOO...N
HEL-LOOO !!
HUH ?!

NEXT: Momma's Coming

DBZ : 48
The Bittersweet End

VWOOO- - - -ON

PSSHHH

VNN---N

GOHAN !!!!
WOPP

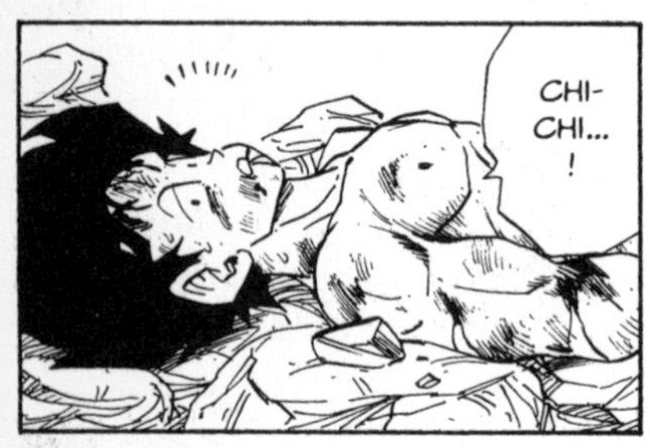
CHI-CHI... !

VOOOM

BOING

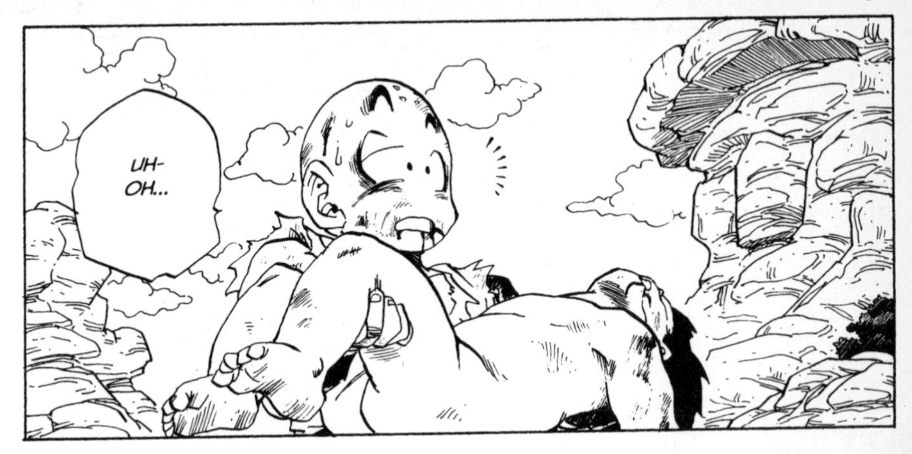
UH-
OH...

GOHAN
!!!
GOHAN
!!!

WAKE UP, BABY!!! WAKE UP!!! MOMMY'S HERE!!!
......
WHAT DID THEY DO TO YOU?!!!

G-GOHAN'S JUST FINE... GOKU'S THE ONE WHO'S REALLY...
SPEAK TO ME

I'M SORRY I LEFT YOU WITH HIM!!!
I'LL NEVER DO IT AGAIN !!!

...UM... CHI-CHI... ?
...YOUR HUSBAND... ?

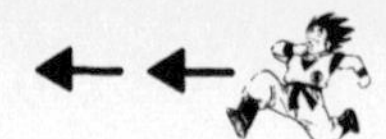

GOKU... ARE YOU OKAY...?
OOO... THIS LOOKS BAD...
T-TMP
T-TMP
THE SAIYAN... GOT AWAY... S...SORRY....

DO NOT BE SORRY FOR SUCH A VICTORY.
...OH... MASTER KARIN...

THERE'S NO WORD FOR POWER LIKE HIS...
B-BULMA... THEY GOT EVERYBODY BUT US FOUR... INCLUDING YAMCHA...

I FIGURED THAT. BUT IT'S OKAY!
WE'LL USE THE DRAGON BALLS IN A YEAR...
AND THEY'LL COME BACK TO LIFE!

UM...

......
RIGHT ?
I-I'M RIGHT, RIGHT... ?!

PICCOLO IS DEAD...
AND SO...
THE DRAGON BALLS...
ARE GONE...

OH C-COME ON...! YOU'RE JOKING, RIGHT... ?!!
Y-YOU SAID FOUR SURVIVED...! S-SO TH-THE OTHER ONE'S GOTTA BE PICCOLO, RIGHT?!

OH, IT DOES, DOES IT?
hmph

N...NO... YOU DON'T MEAN...
YAMCHA...
YAMCHA'S NEVER...
NEVER..... ?!
......

B...
BUT...

WAAAAAH!!!
YOU KNEW... ?
WELL...
YES...

I CAN'T BELIEVE IT...
I JUST ASSUMED... THAT PICCOLO SURVIVED TOO...

WAIT A MINUTE!! I ALMOST GET THE FEELING YOU WISH IT WAS **ME** WHO GOT IT!!
IF I HADN'T BEEN HERE, THESE GUYS'D ALL BE DEAD !!!
WOULD A LITTLE THANK YOU HURT?!

ENOUGH. ENOUGH.
THESE PEOPLE NEED MEDICAL ATTENTION.
AND I HAVE NO MORE "SENZU" BEANS.

...N... !

CAREFUL. CAREFUL.

VVVV....N
CAPSULE
192

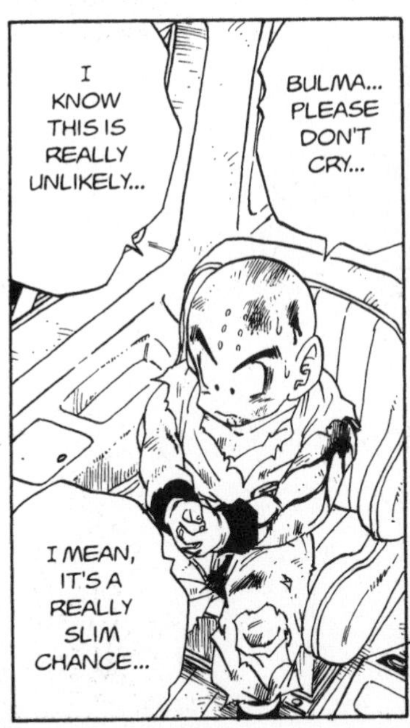
I KNOW THIS IS REALLY UNLIKELY...
BULMA... PLEASE DON'T CRY...
I MEAN, IT'S A REALLY SLIM CHANCE...

A... A LITTLE MORE THAT WAY...
hic SOB
AND THE... BODIES OF THE OTHERS...?

I DON'T WANT TO GET YOUR HOPES UP YET... BUT I THINK THERE MIGHT, MAYBE, BE A POSSIBILITY...
...THAT WE CAN BRING THEM BACK TO LIFE...

WHAT ?!
OF COURSE, I COULD BE GRASPING AT STRAWS....

YOU SAID.... SOMETHING LIKE THAT BEFORE..... WHAT IS IT, KURIRIN...? TELL US WHAT....

WHOA !
HANG ON, I'LL TELL YOU LATER.
DOWN THERE, MASTER... THAT'S WHERE THE BODIES ARE...

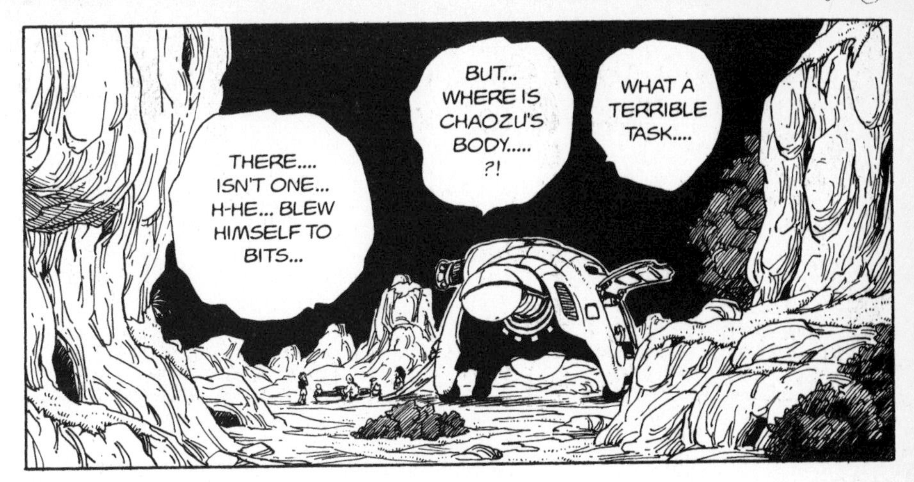
WHAT A TERRIBLE TASK....
BUT... WHERE IS CHAOZU'S BODY..... ?!
THERE.... ISN'T ONE... H-HE... BLEW HIMSELF TO BITS...

I DO WISH WE COULD BRING THEM BACK TO LIFE. THEIR SACRIFICES HAVE BEEN SO GREAT...
I FEEL SUCH RAGE AT MY HELP-LESSNESS...

GO HAVE A GOOD CRY! IT DID WONDERS FOR ME!

VOOOOOSH

...M...
M... MM...

GO-HAN!!
YOU'RE AWAKE ?!

OH !!!

!?
IT'S ALL RIGHT, SWEET-HEART! MOMMA'S HERE!
W... WHAT... ?!

M-MOMMY... !!
OHHH, YOU POOR BAAAAABY!! YOU MUST'VE BEEN SO SCAAAARED...!!

B-BUT THE SAIYAN... ?!
HE... UH.... GOT AWAY... !

BUT WE REALLY TOOK IT OUT OF HIM!
I BET HE NEVER COMES BACK !

IT'S OVER, GOHAN !
HE FOUGHT WELL. YOU SHOULD BE PROUD.

HOW MUCH YOU WANNA--
SAVE IT FOR LATER!!
......

WH- WHERE'S DADDY... ?!

BEHIND YOU, GOHAN...
I'LL BE FINE.... THANKS TO ALL OF YOU...!

DADDY... !
HEH HEH...

HEY, AREN'T YOU THE WIFE ?
SHOW A LITTLE CONCERN, WILL YA ?
WHAT KINDA MARRIAGE IS THIS?

CONCERN?! AFTER HE NEARLY GOT HIS OWN SON KILLED?!!
I'VE TOLD HIM NOT TO DRAG MY BABY INTO--

B-BUT MOM... THE WHOLE EARTH WAS...
OH, WHAT DO I CARE ABOUT THE EARTH?!
GOKU, CAN I HIT HER?

KURIRIN...
SAY WHAT YOU WERE ABOUT TO SAY....

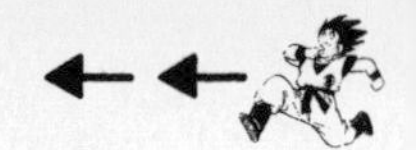

...
OH...
!
R-
RIGHT....
IT'S
JUST...

...THE SAIYANS...
I THINK... FOUND
OUT ABOUT THE
DRAGON BALLS...AND
THEIR WISH-GRANTING
POWERS...THROUGH
GOKU'S BROTHER'S
TRANSMITTER...
...SO THEY
WERE TRYING
TO GET THE
DRAGON BALLS
WHILE THEY
WERE
HERE...

!?
REALLY...
?

YEAH...

BUT... THEY SAID
SOMETHING WEIRD
WHEN THEY SAW
PICCOLO..."HE'S A
NAMEKIAN!" THEY MADE
IT SOUND LIKE PICCOLO...
AND KAMI-SAMA
TOO...WERE
ORIGINALLY ALIENS...

WITH
FACES LIKE
THOSE,
WHO'S
SURPRISED
?!
LET
HIM
SPEAK
!!

THEN
THEY SAID
SOMETHING
ELSE...

"IF WE DON'T GET THEM HERE...WE SHOULD JUST GO THERE..."
192
I'M NOT SURE... BUT IT WAS SOMETHING LIKE, "SO IT'S TRUE THAT THERE ARE GLOBES THAT GRANT WISHES ON THE PLANET NAMEK"...

THAT'S THE BIG SECRET ?
PFFT.

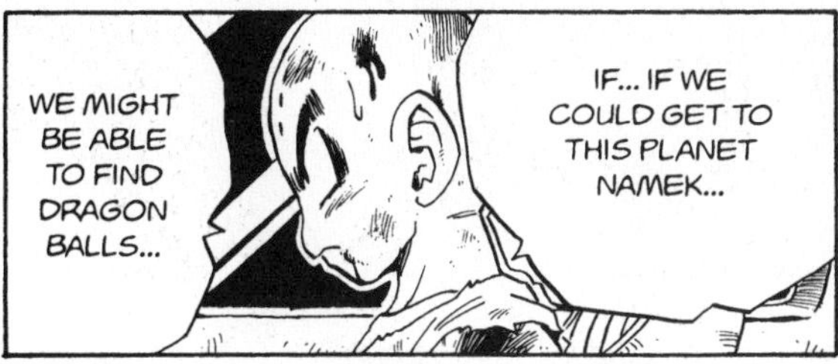
WE MIGHT BE ABLE TO FIND DRAGON BALLS...
IF... IF WE COULD GET TO THIS PLANET NAMEK...

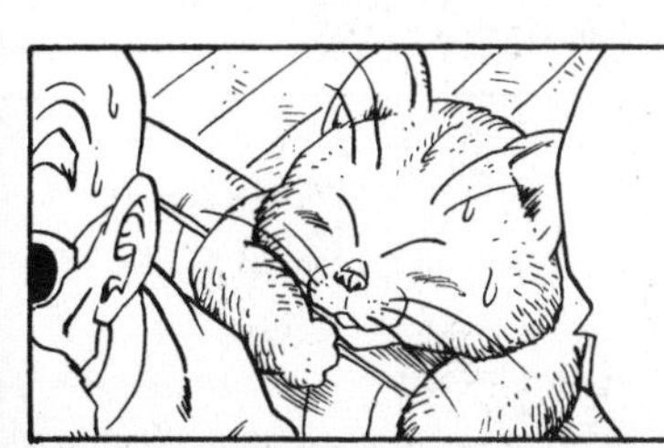
...AND THEN EVERYONE WHO DIED COULD BE RESTORED TO LIFE...!!

I...I THINK I HEARD THAT TOO....
I DID!! NAMEKIANS HAVE POWERS TO MAKE MAGIC BALLS...!!

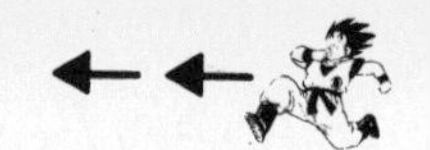

AND OUR DRAGON BALLS WOULD COME BACK TOO!
THAT'S RIGHT! AND IF PICCOLO CAME BACK TO LIFE, SO WOULD KAMI-SAMA...!!

PICCOLO WOULD COME BACK TO LIFE TOO!!
G-GOHAN, WHAT ARE YOU SAYING ?!!

ANOTHER PLANET...? IT'S FANTASTIC...IT'S IMPOSSIBLE.....
Y'MEAN... THAT'S YOUR ONE HOPE... ?
OH, COME ON, BULMA !

OH...

KURIRIN... HOW ARE YOU EVEN GOING TO FIND OUT WHERE THIS WHAT'S-IT PLANET IS?

I HAVE A FEELING HE'LL KNOW...
LEAVE IT TO ME... I CAN CONTACT THE LORD OF WORLDS THROUGH MY MIND...

IT COULD WORK!! IT REALLY COULD!!
HA HA HA!!

NEXT: All Aboard...for Planet Namek!

DBZ:49 • Destination Namek

VOOONNNN

KAIŌ-SAMA... YOU WERE LISTENING. DO YOU KNOW...
...WHERE THIS PLANET NAMEK IS?

PLANET NAMEK? OF COURSE I KNOW.
WHY DO YOU THINK THEY CALL ME THE LORD OF WORLDS?

!!
H-H-HEY... I CAN HEAR HIM TOO?!
OKAY. THIS IS A TRICK... ISN'T IT?

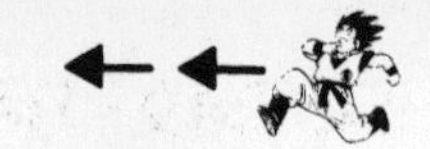

LORD OF WORLDS...
THEY'RE ALL LISTENING. TELL US, PLEASE.

FIRST, LET ME SAY ONE THING... YOU DID VERY WELL!
WHEN SON GOKU WENT DOWN, I HONESTLY THOUGHT IT WAS OVER. I'M IMPRESSED, REALLY!

I DIDN'T EXPECT HIM TO BE SO POWERFUL.
NOT EVEN THE KAIŌ-KEN DID MUCH AGAINST HIM.

WELL...*AHEM*... YES. VEGETA'S POWER WAS A BIT OF A MISCALCU-LATION ON MY PART AS WELL.
ACTUALLY, A PRETTY BIG MISCALCU-LATION...

D-DID I MAKE A MISTAKE... IN LETTING HIM ESCAPE...?
...WELL... FRANKLY ...

WHOA, WHOA, WHOA! YOU DON'T MEAN GOKU DID IT ON PURPOSE ?!
I'LL... UH...TELL YOU ABOUT IT LATER...

YOU DO THAT.
NOW, ABOUT NAMEK'S POSITION... IN EARTH TERMS, LET'S SEE... IT'S BEARING SUB3... 9045YX...

"TURTLE BOY"...?
HEY, TURTLE BOY, TAKE OVER FOR ME! I'VE GOTTA DO SOME CALCULATIONS...!

DON'T TELL ME YOU KNOW WHAT THAT MEANS, BULMA?!
N-9045... YX...!

...THE PLANET DOES SEEM TO BE GOING BACK TO THE WAY IT USED TO BE...
PLANET NAMEK WAS ONCE A PARADISE... BUT, IF I'M NOT CONFUSING IT WITH SOME OTHER PLACE, IT SUFFERED A CLIMATIC CATACLYSM LONG AGO... ACTUALLY, I THOUGHT THE NAMEKIANS ALL DIED OFF AT THE TIME... HMM...
BUT HOW COULD ANY OF THEM HAVE SURVIVED...?

I HAVE A BAD FEELING ABOUT THIS...
pi pi pi piiiiii

I'LL JUST HAVE TO CHECK UP ON THE PLANET...
NOW, NOW. DON'T JUMP TO CONCLUSIONS.
...WHICH WAY IS IT AGAIN...?

Y'MEAN IT'S NO GOOD?! THERE WON'T BE NO DRAGON BALLS?!

OHHH, NO...

AH! THIS WAY!
LET'S SEE...
......

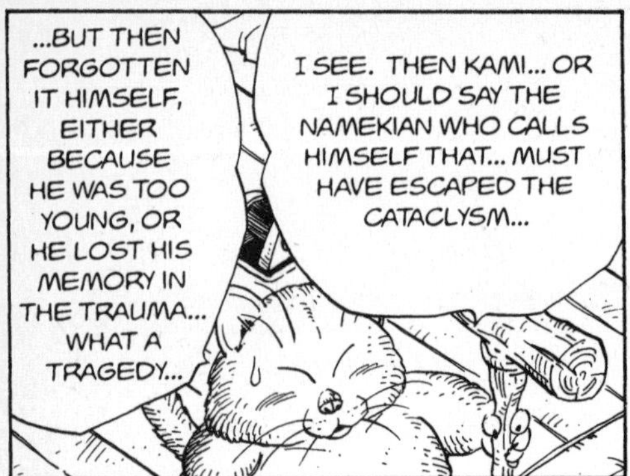
I SEE. THEN KAMI... OR I SHOULD SAY THE NAMEKIAN WHO CALLS HIMSELF THAT... MUST HAVE ESCAPED THE CATACLYSM...
...BUT THEN FORGOTTEN IT HIMSELF, EITHER BECAUSE HE WAS TOO YOUNG, OR HE LOST HIS MEMORY IN THE TRAUMA... WHAT A TRAGEDY...

B-B-BUT DRAGON BALLS GRANT ANY WISH, RIGHT?!
SO IF THE NAMEKIANS COULD MAKE THOSE THINGS, HOW COME THEY COULDN'T USE 'EM TO STOP THE CATECHISM ?!

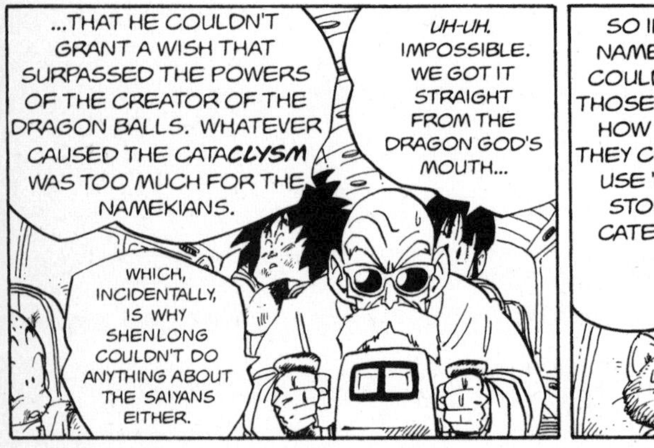
UH-UH. IMPOSSIBLE. WE GOT IT STRAIGHT FROM THE DRAGON GOD'S MOUTH...
...THAT HE COULDN'T GRANT A WISH THAT SURPASSED THE POWERS OF THE CREATOR OF THE DRAGON BALLS. WHATEVER CAUSED THE CATA*CLYSM* WAS TOO MUCH FOR THE NAMEKIANS.
WHICH, INCIDENTALLY, IS WHY SHENLONG COULDN'T DO ANYTHING ABOUT THE SAIYANS EITHER.

AND I THOUGHT DRAGON BALLS WERE SUPPOSED TO BE SO HOT !
WHAT A CROCK!

OH, DEAR L-- I MEAN, DEAR *ME!!* THEY'RE *THERE!* THE NAMEKIANS ARE *THERE* !!
THERE ARE ONLY ABOUT A HUNDRED OF THEM... BUT THEY'VE SURVIVED... AND THEY'RE THRIVING AGAIN !!

!!

YES!!!

GACK! A H-H-HUNDRED OF THOSE GUYS...?

DON'T WORRY. NAMEKIANS ARE A MOSTLY PEACEFUL RACE...JUST LIKE KAMI-SAMA OF EARTH WAS. THE GREAT DEMON PICCOLO WAS MOST LIKELY CORRUPTED BY THE MALICIOUS HUMANS HE MET ALONG THE WAY...

YEAH. I GUESS THERE'S BAD IN EVERY RACE...EVEN HUMANS.
LOOK WHO'S TALKING...

HANG ON...DOES THIS MEAN THAT NOT ONLY KAMI-SAMA COULD RETURN TO LIFE... BUT YAMCHA AND TENSHINHAN COULD TOO?!

I ADMIRE YOUR OPTIMISM...
BUT IT WON'T GO AS EASY AS THAT!

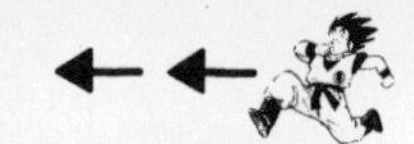

HUH ?!

WE KNOW WHERE PLANET NAMEK IS. BUT HOW ARE WE GOING TO GET THERE?
H-HOW...? W-WITH A SPACESHIP, OF COURSE...

THAT'S PRECISELY WHAT I'M SAYING!
I CALCULATED THE TIME IT WOULD TAKE TO REACH NAMEK ON A SPACE-SHIP WITH THE FASTEST ENGINE MY DAD'S MADE... WHICH WOULD BE THE FASTEST IN THE WORLD.

ANY-BODY WANT TO TAKE A GUESS? NO?
TRY 4339 YEARS AND 3 MONTHS !!
HOPE NOBODY'S IN A HURRY...

F-F-FOUR... THOUSAND... ?!

LORD OF WORLDS...
WHAT SHOULD WE DO...?

WELL... HMM... UH...
THAT'S AN AWFULLY GOOD QUESTION...

SHHHH

HEH HEH !
WHAT'S EVERY-BODY SO SAD ABOUT ?!

?
LET'S JUST USE THE SAIYANS' SPACE-SHIPS !

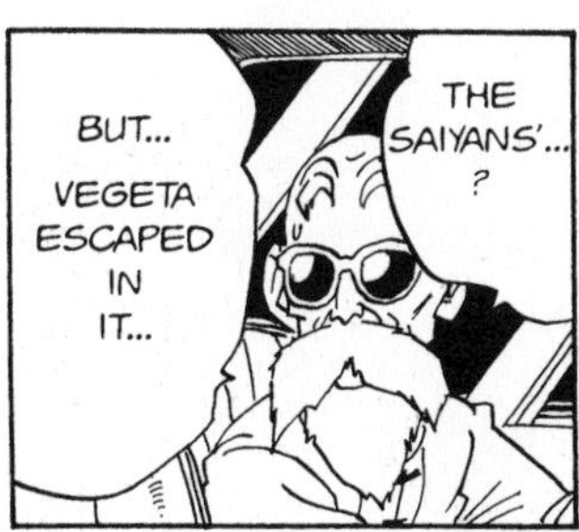
THE SAIYANS'... ?
BUT... VEGETA ESCAPED IN IT...

YEAH. IN A LITTLE TINY SHIP THAT HADDA BE FOR *ONE!* THAT MEANS HIS DEAD BUDDY'S SHIP MUST STILL BE SOMEWHERE!

YEAH! YEAH! THERE WAS THE ONE MY BROTHER CAME ON, TOO...!
EXCEPT... THAT ONE WAS BROKEN...
BY GOHAN...

BUT THERE'S AT LEAST ONE, THEN!
IF WE CAN FIND IT AND ANALYZE IT, MAYBE WE CAN USE IT!!

IT'S PROBABLY AT THE EASTERN CITY... THE FIRST PLACE THE SAIYANS DESTROYED!
LET'S GO LOOK FOR IT, RIGHT NOW!

I THOUGHT IT'D BE USEFUL, SO I PICKED THIS UP....
I THINK IT'S WHAT VEGETA PRESSED TO CALL HIS SPACESHIP! MUST BE SOME KINDA REMOTE CONTROL!

W-WE CAN DO IT! WE CAN DO IT!
HEH HEH... HEH HEH...

HA HA HA!!! YES!!!
HOPE, AT LAST!!!

THE NEXT DAY... AT THE WESTERN CITY HOSPITAL...

WELL, THAT'S NOT EXACTLY WHAT I WANTED TO HEAR. FOUR MONTHS FOR MY INJURIES TO HEAL, THEY SAID!
AND I MIGHT ***NEVER*** GET BACK TO NORMAL...

OH, THERE'S NOTHING TO WORRY ABOUT.
IN ANOTHER MONTH THERE'LL BE SOME NEW SENZU ON ITS TREE.

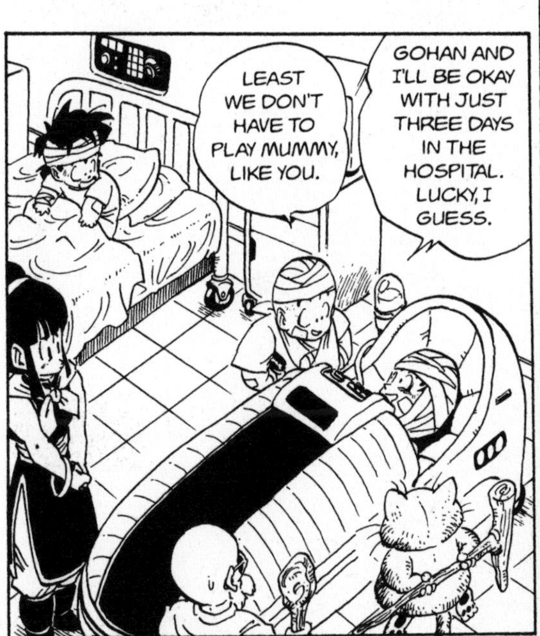
GOHAN AND I'LL BE OKAY WITH JUST THREE DAYS IN THE HOSPITAL. LUCKY, I GUESS.
LEAST WE DON'T HAVE TO PLAY MUMMY, LIKE YOU.

HMPH...
I WENT THROUGH ALL THAT AND I DON'T EVEN GET TO BE HOSPITALIZED!
ARE YOU THAT DESPERATE FOR HOSPITAL FOOD?

AFTER YOU WENT THROUGH ALL *WHAT*, YAJIROBE?
BEGGING THE SAIYAN TO FORGIVE YOU AND LET YOU JOIN THEIR GANG?
OR DID I DREAM THAT?

YA WANNA GET BEAT UP, BALDY?!
THAT WAS JUST A STRAJATEM TO TRICK 'EM!
AH, YOUR "STRAJATEMS"!

FORGET IT, FORGET IT.
YOU SAVED THE EARTH. YOU SURVIVED. AND MAYBE THOSE WHO DIED CAN RETURN TO LIFE TOO. IT'S ENOUGH.

HEY!!
EVERY-BODY CHECK OUT WHAT'S ON TV!!
CAPSULE

YOU SCARED ME, BULMA!
I THOUGHT FOR A SECOND YOU WERE SOME PSYCHOTIC NURSE...
CH HK
OH, SHUT UP! JUST LOOK AT THE TV !

...SCIENTISTS CONJECTURE THAT THE GLOBULAR OBJECT UNEARTHED IN THE RUINED EASTERN CITY...
...MAY BE A VESSEL OF EXTRATER-RESTRIAL ORIGIN.

AH-HA!!
THAT'S IT!! THE SAIYANS' SHIP!!

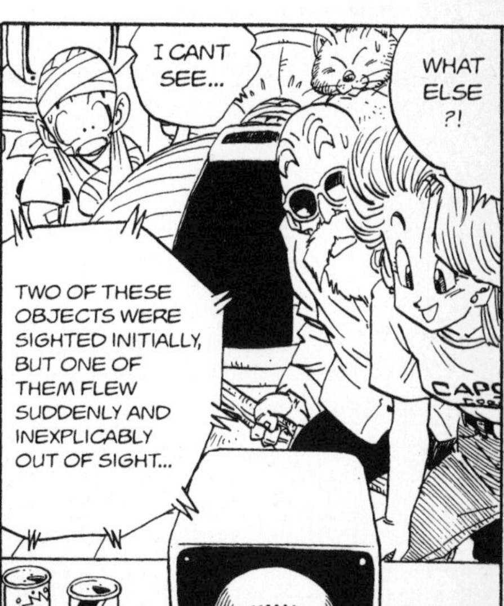
WHAT ELSE ?!
I CANT SEE...
TWO OF THESE OBJECTS WERE SIGHTED INITIALLY, BUT ONE OF THEM FLEW SUDDENLY AND INEXPLICABLY OUT OF SIGHT...

THIS ISN'T GOOD...
IF THOSE SCIENTISTS HAVE ALREADY FOUND IT...

THAT MAKES IT MORE FUN !
THINK OF THE LOOKS ON THEIR FACES WHEN KURIRIN'S REMOTE CONTROL SENDS IT ZOOMING AWAY!

DO YOU THINK IT'LL ACTUALLY WORK...?
KURIRIN. WHO'S THE GENIUS IN THIS ROOM?
I CHECKED OUT ALL THE CONTROLS LAST NIGHT!

JUST WATCH! WE'LL BE ABLE TO SEE IT ON LIVE TV!
A BLIP HERE... A BEEP THERE...

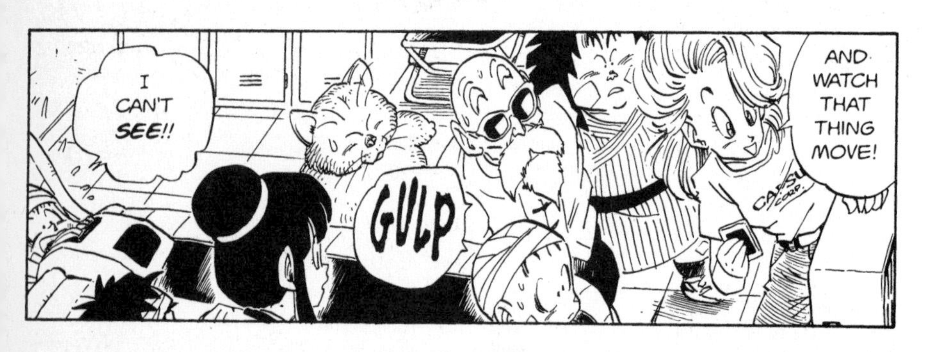
AND WATCH THAT THING MOVE!
GULP
I CAN'T SEE!!
CAPSULE CORP.

DOOM

HUH ?!
CAPSULE CORP.

SOMETHING'S HAPPENED...! THE OBJECT...IT'S SUDDENLY EXPLODED!! THE REMAINS OF THE SPACECRAFT, IF SUCH IT WAS, ARE SCATTERED EVERYWHERE...!
CAPSULE

OHHHH, SHOOT !!!
I TOLD MYSELF, "DON'T TOUCH THE SELF-DESTRUCT BUTTON"!

THE... THE LAST HOPE...
IS NOW TOTALLY SUNK.

IT'S...
IT'S ALL OVER...

KONG HOSPITAL
...

THERE'S... THERE'S NOTHING TO DO...
NOT EVEN KINTO'UN... COULD CARRY US FAST ENOUGH...

YOU HAD TO PICK UP THAT STUPID REMOTE CONTROL!
YOU HAD TO PRESS THE STUPID SELF-DESTRUCT BUTTON !

EXCUSE MR. POPO.
WAH!!!

EEEP!!

MR. PUH-PUH-PUH---
INDEED.

SOME-ONE COME.
THERE IS A SPACE-SHIP.
HUH ?!

NEXT: What Th'?!

DBZ : 50 • The Mysterious Spaceship

YOU'RE KIDDING!! TH-THERE'S REALLY ANOTHER SPACESHIP... ?!
PROBABLY.

WHO'S THIS GUY ?
IT'S MR. POPO.
HE LIVES AT KAMI-SAMA'S CASTLE.
AND SAYS HE HAS SINCE BEFORE THE CURRENT KAMI-SAMA AND THE ONE BEFORE THAT AND THE ONE BEFORE THAT....
BACK UP, BACK UP. "PROBABLY"... ?

PROBABLY A SPACESHIP. BUT MR. POPO CANNOT BE SURE.
IF SOME-ONE COMES, MR. POPO WILL GUIDE HIM.

BULMA !
ME ?!

WHO ELSE COULD FIGURE OUT AN ALIEN SPACE-SHIP?

I-I-I DON'T KNOW ABOUT THIS...
DON'T YOU THINK THIS GUY HAS KINDA SHIFTY EYES... ?

WELL...JUST BE CAREFUL!! I'M NOT LIKE THEM-- I'M A DELICATE LI'L GIRLIE!
YOU CAN'T CHICKEN OUT ON US NOW, BULMA!!
HOSPITAL

MR. POPO IS OFF.
SLOWLY, SLOWLY !!

VNNNN

UM...I DON'T SUPPOSE ANYONE KNOWS HOW HE DID THAT...
IF THERE'S REALLY A SPACESHIP... WHOSE IS IT?

!!
VNNN

HWOO---OO
WE ARE HERE. GET OFF MR. POPO.
HUH?! A-ALREADY ?!

B-BUT WHERE ARE WE...?!
THE BIGGEST FREEZER KNOWN TO MAN?!!

YUNZABIT HIGHLANDS.
Y-YUNZABIT...?!

THAT'S THE FARTHEST CORNER OF THE EARTH!!
Y-YOU MEAN TO TELL ME THAT IN THAT INSTANT...
NOW, LET MR. POPO SEE....

WAS IT THIS WAY?
WHOA! WAIT! TIME OUT!
YOU EXPECT ME TO BELIEVE THERE'S A SPACESHIP IN A PLACE LIKE THIS?!

OH, I GET IT...
DRAG THE LUSCIOUS BABE OUT WHERE NOBODY CAN SEE WHAT YOU'RE GONNA DO TO HER, EH?!

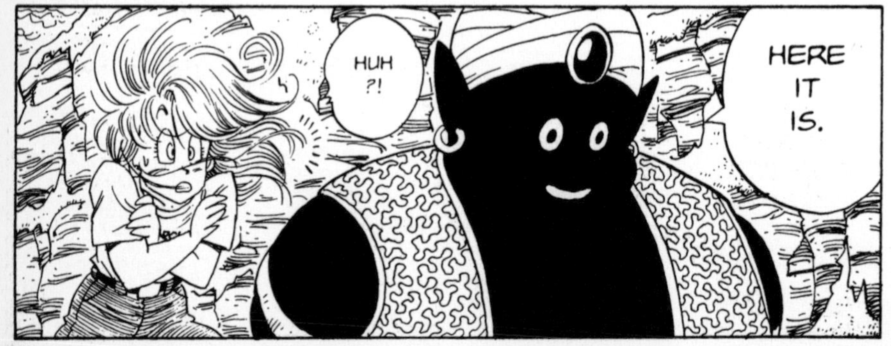
HERE IT IS.
HUH?!

WAK !!

IS IT A SPACE-SHIP ?
UHHH... LEMME GET BACK TO YOU ON THAT...

CAPSULE CORPORATION

TMP

TONG
TONG

WH-WHAT IS THIS...? IT'S NOT METAL...
I'VE NEVER SEEN ANYTHING LIKE IT...

OKAY, ENOUGH O' THE POPO MYSTERY THEATER!
EXACTLY WHAT DO YOU KNOW ABOUT THIS?!

A CENTURY AGO, THE LORD KAMI-SAMA SPOKE OF HIS GODLY PAST TO MR. POPO...FOR THE FIRST AND ONLY TIME.
IT WAS A MYSTERIOUS TALE. KAMI-SAMA SAID THAT HIS GODSHIP HAD LIVED IN THE YUNZABIT HIGHLANDS AS A CHILD. THEN MR. POPO SAID THAT THE YUNZABIT IS A WASTELAND. WHY WOULD A CHILD BE THERE?

AND...?
KAMI-SAMA SAID THAT HIS GODSHIP DID NOT KNOW. EVEN HIS LORDLY MIND WAS CONFUSED. PERHAPS THE GODLY HEAD HAD BEEN STRUCK AND HIS HOLY MEMORY LOST....

MR. POPO ASKED AGAIN: WERE HIS GODSHIP'S PARENTS THERE?
KAMI-SAMA REPLIED: NO PARENTS. ONLY A NOTE READING, "WE WILL COME FOR YOU LATER. WAIT FOR US..."

LOOK, I'M NOT GOOD AT SUSPENSEFUL NARRATIVES!
JUST TELL ME WHERE THIS IS GOING, OKAY?!

THE LORD KAMI-SAMA WAITED FOR HIS HOLY PARENTS FOR A LONG TIME. AND WAITED AND WAITED....

THERE WAS A HOUSE THERE... I TRUSTED THAT MY PARENTS WOULD COME... SOMEDAY...
BUT THE YEARS STRETCHED ON... AND NO ONE CAME. IT WAS HARD... FINDING FOOD WAS HARD...

HOW LONG DID I WAIT? 20 YEARS? 30?
FINALLY, I GAVE UP AND LEFT THE HOUSE... AND YUNZABIT...
I RETURNED THERE FROM TIME TO TIME TO SEE IF THERE WAS ANY SIGN... BUT NOTHING CHANGED...

UM...DID I FORGET TO ASK... WHERE'S THIS GOING?!
MORTALS ARE SO IMPATIENT. MR. POPO COMES TO THE POINT...

IT DIDN'T OCCUR TO ME AT THE TIME...
I DIDN'T KNOW ANY OTHER HOUSES, AFTER ALL...

BUT AS I CAME TO KNOW DIFFERENT WORLDS, I REALIZED WHAT AN ODD HOUSE THAT WAS.
IT WAS ROUND AND HAD 4 LEGS... VERY MUCH LIKE SOME SORT OF CREATURE... THERE WAS NO KNOB OR LOCK ON THE DOOR, AND IT OPENED WITH A SPOKEN WORD...

"PICCOLO."

PPPP-- !!
CAPSULE CORPORATION

VRRRR

THEN THIS--
THIS--- !!

GO IN.

TH-THIS IS KAMI-SAMA'S HOUSE... !!
SAY IT AGAIN, AND IT CLOSES. "PICCOLO."
VNNNNNN

SLAM
!!

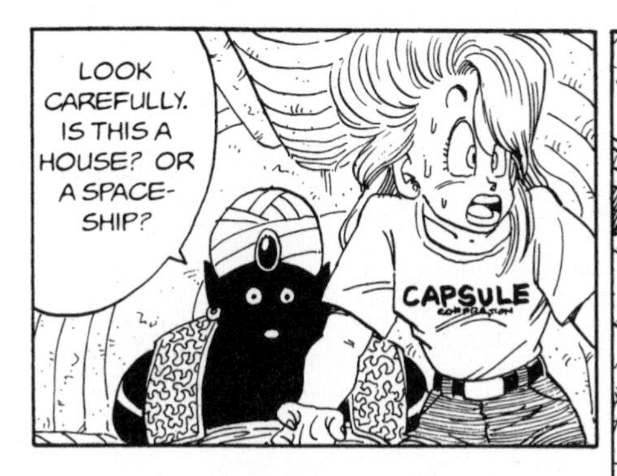
LOOK CAREFULLY. IS THIS A HOUSE? OR A SPACE-SHIP?
CAPSULE CORPORATION

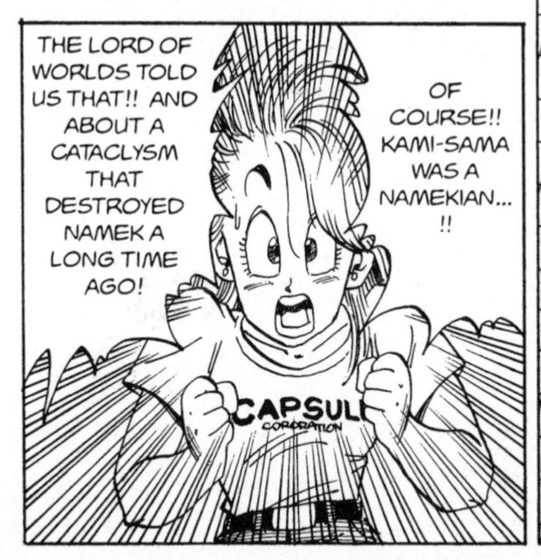
OF COURSE!! KAMI-SAMA WAS A NAMEKIAN... !!
THE LORD OF WORLDS TOLD US THAT!! AND ABOUT A CATACLYSM THAT DESTROYED NAMEK A LONG TIME AGO!
CAPSULE CORPORATION

MR. POPO ALSO HEARD THE LORD OF WORLDS SPEAK. THEN MR. POPO REMEMBERED THE STORY ABOUT THIS HOUSE.
MR. POPO THOUGHT THAT PERHAPS IT WAS WORTH TAKING A LOOK FOR THIS HOUSE...
I-IF THIS IS A SPACESHIP, THEN HIS STORY MAKES TOTAL SENSE...
!

WHEN PLANET NAMEK WAS IN DANGER, KAMI-SAMA'S HOLY PARENTS PUT HIS GODSHIP ON BOARD AND FLEW HIM TO EARTH...
FOR SOME REASON THEY COULDN'T COME UNTIL LATER... AND THEN SOMETHING WENT WRONG... THEY...THEY NEVER MADE IT....

THAT'S GOTTA BE IT!
CAPSULE
'CAUSE I NEVER SAW ANY HOUSE LIKE THIS!
IT'S GOTTA BE A SHIP...!

B-BUT...
HOW DO WE USE IT...?

THE DOOR'S WORKING, SO THERE MUST BE SOME POWER...
IS THIS... THE MAIN SWITCH? NO...
UM... THIS ONE IS...

HMM... THAT'S NOT IT EITHER...
THIS IS WEIRD... I WONDER IF THERE'S A PASSCODE OR SOME-THING...
YEAH! IF IT WAS TOO EASY TO WORK, KAMI-SAMA WOULD'VE MESSED WITH IT WHEN HE WAS LITTLE!

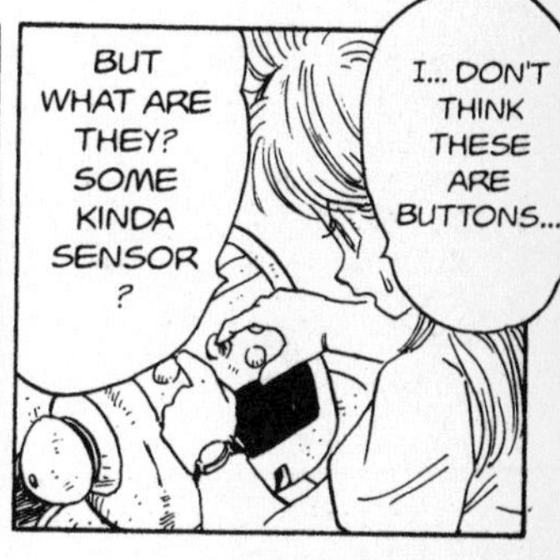
I... DON'T THINK THESE ARE BUTTONS...
BUT WHAT ARE THEY? SOME KINDA SENSOR ?

!!

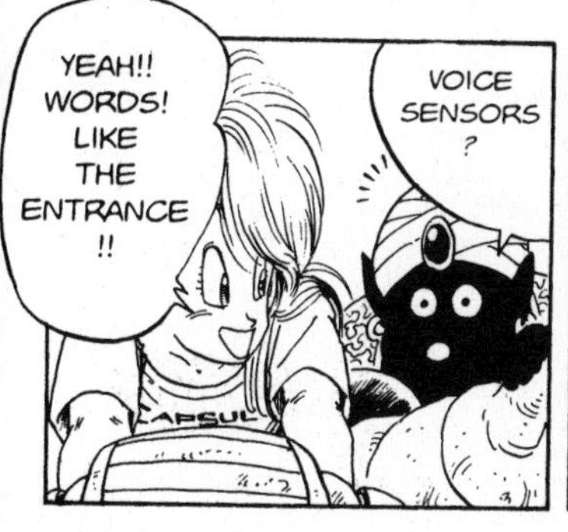
VOICE SENSORS ?
YEAH!! WORDS! LIKE THE ENTRANCE !!

WHAT TO SAY? "PICCOLO" ?
NO! THAT'S GOTTA BE JUST TO GET IN AND OUT!

MOVE!! CAN YOU HEAR ME?! FLY !!
ZOOM!! LIFT!! ZIP!! TRAVEL!!

SHH~-HH

IT'S NO USE... IT WOULDN'T BE IN AN EARTH LANGUAGE. TOO BAD NOBODY KNOWS NAMEKIAN...
KAMI-SAMA AND PICCOLO WERE TALKING IN SOME STRANGE LANGUAGE AT THE MARTIAL ARTS TOUR-NAMENT...
THAT MUST'VE BEEN NAMEKIAN.

IF THAT WAS NAMEKIAN...
...THEN MR. POPO KNOWS IT!

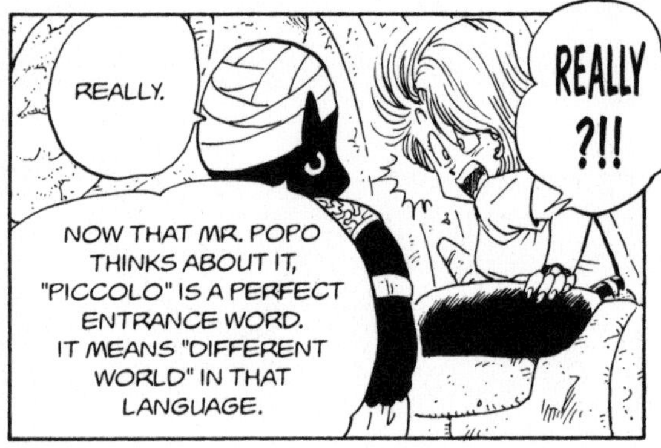
REALLY ?!!
REALLY.
NOW THAT MR. POPO THINKS ABOUT IT, "PICCOLO" IS A PERFECT ENTRANCE WORD. IT MEANS "DIFFERENT WORLD" IN THAT LANGUAGE.

SO THE GREAT DEMON PICCOLO MEANS....
OH, WHO CARES?! WHY DIDN'T YOU TELL ME YOU SPOKE NAMEKIAN ?!

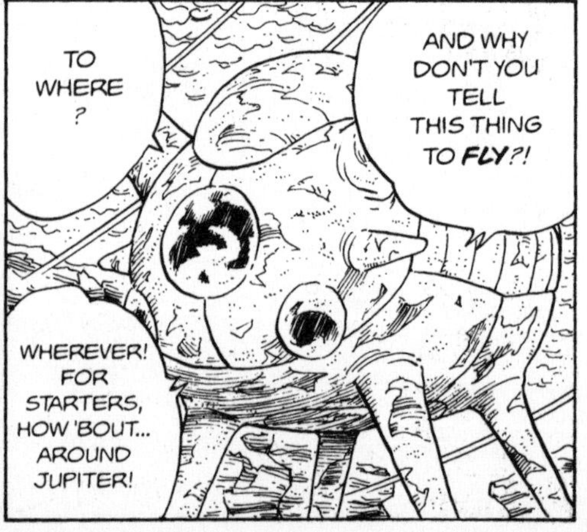
AND WHY DON'T YOU TELL THIS THING TO ***FLY***?!
TO WHERE ?
WHEREVER! FOR STARTERS, HOW 'BOUT... AROUND JUPITER!

piiii
!!
IT SAYS "ROGER" !!

GYNNNN
CAPSULE

AAAAA!!!
VOOONNN

NNNNNN

.....

YYYYYYYYUP.... THAT'S JUPITER, ALL RIGHT!
I HOPE YOU DON'T THINK I'M BEING PREMATURE IN SAYING....

WE DID IT !!!!
YES. YES, INDEED.

MR. POPO IS GLAD.
NOW KAMI-SAMA MAY COME BACK TO LIFE...

NEXT: Take-off!!

KONG HOSPITAL
...
...AND SO THE SPACESHIP IS PERFECT!!
WITH THAT, WE CAN GET TO PLANET NAMEK IN JUST ONE MONTH! WE'LL JUST HAVE TO REVAMP THE INTERIOR A LITTLE...
AND WE CAN TAKE OFF IN 5 DAYS!!
THAT IS RIGHT.
CAPSULE CORPORATION

DBZ:51 • 3...2...1...Lift Off!

GOING TO PLANET NAMEK ON KAMI-SAMA'S SHIP!! THAT'S AWESOME!!
THE FAINT GLIMMER OF HOPE IS ABOUT TO BECOME REALITY!
SO, MR. POPO, WE'LL LEAVE GOING TO PLANET NAMEK TO YOU!!
HUH ?
MR. POPO ISN'T GOING.

WHAT?! B-BUT !!
YOU'RE THE ONLY ONE WHO UNDERSTANDS NAMEKIAN!! AND YOU LOOK TOUGH!! THE ONLY WAY IS FOR YOU TO GO!!
CAPSULE CORPORATION

MR. POPO CAN'T GO. THERE WOULD BE NOBODY AT KAMI-SAMA'S CASTLE FOR 2 MONTHS; NO GOOD.
DON'T WORRY, MR. POPO WILL TEACH NAMEKIAN.

THEN YOU WOULD HAVE TO GO, BULMA.
YOU'RE THE ONLY ONE KNOW-LEDGEABLE ABOUT MECHANICS IF SOME-THING GOES WRONG.

...A-ALL RIGHT... IT DOESN'T SOUND TOO DANGER-OUS...
MUMBLE MUMBLE
...I'LL HAVE TO ADD A SHOWER ROOM... A MORE COM-FORTABLE BED, AND A STEREO...
CAPSULE CORPORATION

BUT I DON'T WANT TO GO ALONE! SOMEONE COME WITH ME!

YOU'RE NOT GOING TO GET ME TO GO!!
NOBODY EXPECTED YOU TO.

2 MONTHS ROUND TRIP... ALL RIGHT! OH WELL, I'LL GO!
THAT'LL JUST ADD NEED-LESS DANGER !!

SON'S IN NO SHAPE...
KURIRIN! YOU'LL COME WITH ME, WON'T YOU ?!

WHAT? M-ME ?
W-WELL, ALL RIGHT... 2 MONTHS... I'D WANTED TO TRAIN...
WE DON'T KNOW WHEN THE SAIYAN IS COMING BACK...

LUCKY YOU. I WANT TO GO TOO.

I WANTED TO SEE WHAT PLANET NAMEK'S SHENLONG LOOKED LIKE...

WELL, YOU TAKE IT EASY AND WORK OUT COUNTER-MEASURES AGAINST THE SAIYAN.
YEAH... WE'RE COUNTING ON YOU TWO.

T-TAKE ME
WITH YOU...! PLEASE...

G-GOHAN...
WH-WHAT KIND OF SILLY JOKE ARE YOU MAKING...?

IT'S NOT A JOKE.
I-I SERIOUSLY WANT TO GO.

I'M SORRY... I... WANT TO GO, NO MATTER WHAT... I WANT TO... BRING PICCOLO BACK TO LIFE WITH MY OWN HANDS...
D-DON'T BE RIDICULOUS... T-TWO MONTHS, ON TOP OF ALL THIS...
B-BEST KEEP AWAY...

THERE'S NO NEED FOR GOHAN TO DO THAT!! WHAT IF SOMETHING WERE TO HAPPEN?!
WHAT KIND OF NONSENSE ARE YOU TWO TALKING ABOUT?!!
...I SEE.
GOOD FOR YOU, GOHAN.

...
YOU'RE A LITTLE KID!! YOU SHOULD ACT LIKE ONE!!
WHO CARES ABOUT PICCOLO?!

2 MONTHS!! AFTER AN ENTIRE YEAR OF WORRYING!!
WHAT ABOUT CRAM SCHOOL?! YOUR LESSONS?! YOU'RE WAY BEHIND ALL THE OTHER KIDS ALREADY!!
I WON'T ALLOW IT, I ABSOLUTELY FORBID IT!!!

BE QUIET!!!!

OOOOOH

M-MY LITTLE BOY...
H-HAS BECOME A DELINQUENT...

M-MOM... NOW... NOW'S NOT THE TIME TO BE SAYING SUCH THINGS...
EVERYONE... WE ALL FOUGHT FOR THE EARTH... WE HAVE TO BRING THOSE WHO DIED BACK TO LIFE... AND FIGHT THE SAIYAN AGAIN...

I CAN... I CAN FIGHT TOO...!
I HAVE TO DO SOME-THING... !!

HEE HEE. THAT KID SAYS GOOD STUFF SOME-TIMES.

YOU LOSE, CHI-CHI...
LET GOHAN FLY INTO SPACE WITH YOUR BLESSING.

GOHAN...
I'M PROUD OF YOU. YOU'VE GOTTEN SO STRONG...

IT'LL BE FINE! LEAVE IT TO US; THERE'S NOTHING DANGEROUS !
LET'S SEE NOW... WE'LL RE-INPUT THE NAMEKIAN LANGUAGE... AND MEET AT THE TURTLE HOUSE IN 10 DAYS!!
CAPSULE

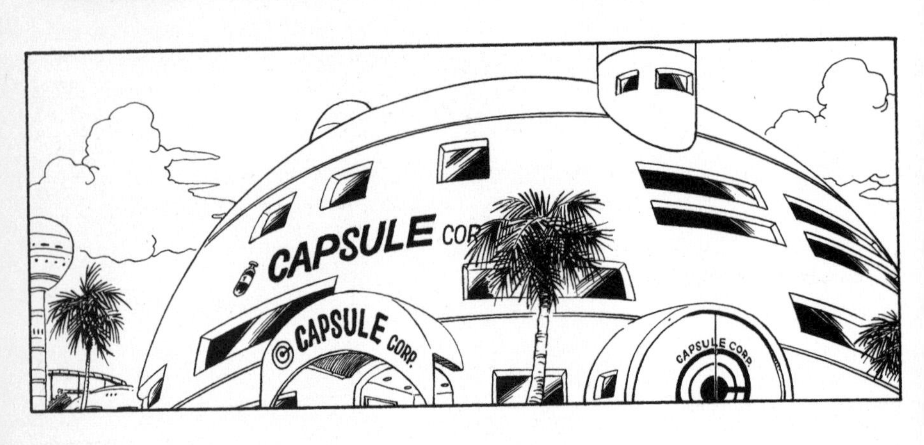

CAPSULE COR
CAPSULE CORP.
CAPSULE CORP.

THIS IS REALLY AMAZING! THE UNIVERSE IS VAST. I GUESS THERE ARE SMARTER GENIUSES THAN ME.
DON'T JUST BE IMPRESSED; HELP ME, DAD!

AND FINALLY, THE DAY OF DEPARTURE...
KAME HOUSE

WOW...
B-BULMA, CAN WE REALLY GO INTO SPACE IN THIS THING?

K-KURIRIN, WHAT A NICE OUTFIT YOU HAVE...
AREN'T YOU UNDERESTIMATING OUTER SPACE...? I EVEN CUT MY HAIR BECAUSE IT WOULD GET IN THE WAY OF MY SPACESUIT...
MUMBLE GRUMBLE
HUH ?
KURIRIN

...AND WHERE'S GOHAN?
OH, HE CALLED TO SAY THAT HE WAS GOING TO SEE GOKU, AND THEN COME RIGHT OVER.

SAY BULMA, SHOULD WE TAKE AN UMBRELLA? PLANET NAMEK MIGHT NOT HAVE GOOD WEATHER, RIGHT?
WHAT-EVER YOU WANT.

OH! LOOKS LIKE THEY'RE HERE!

BYOOO--

SORRY WE'RE A LITTLE LATE!

HOO-WHEE. SO THIS IS A SPACE-SHIP! AMAZING!
NOW THEN GOHAN, BE CAREFUL!

BE SURE TO BRUSH YOUR TEETH AFTER MEALS!
THUD
O-OK...

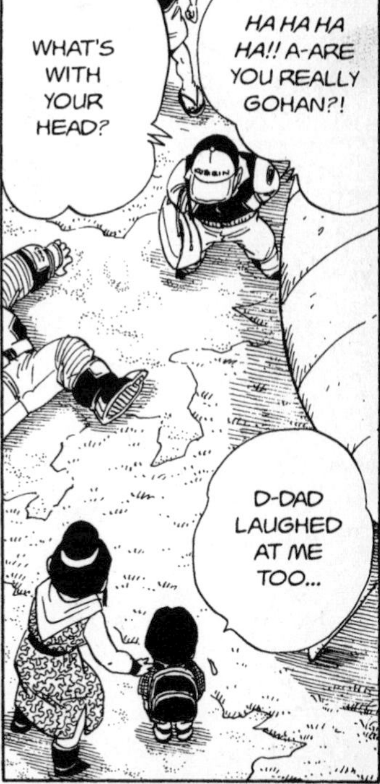
HA HA HA HA!! A-ARE YOU REALLY GOHAN?!
WHAT'S WITH YOUR HEAD?
D-DAD LAUGHED AT ME TOO...

YOU'RE GOING INTO SPACE WHERE NO MAN HAS GONE BEFORE. YOU'LL HAVE TO BE ON YOUR BEST BEHAVIOR.

W-WE BETTER GET GOING...
I FEEL WASHED OUT...

WE'RE COUNTING ON YOU! BE SURE TO FIND THE DRAGON BALLS.
YES !!

GRANDPA, MOM, TURTLE HERMIT AND MR. TURTLE, I'M OFF! TAKE CARE.
WRITE ME EVERY-DAY!
WHIRR
...

THIS IS REALLY EXCITING.
WOW !

BULMA, WHERE SHOULD WE PUT OUR BAGS?
ANYWHERE! HURRY UP AND SIT DOWN!!

LOOKS LIKE SHE'S IN A BAD MOOD...
...?

5 SECONDS
TO TAKE OFF.
DESTINATION:
PLANET
NAMEK!
Peep
OK!

ZOOM

B-BULMA, WE HAVEN'T F-FASTENED OUR SEAT-BELTS YET!!
KURIRIN

WH-WHAT SPEED! I-I CAN'T SEE THEM ANYMORE!
GOHAN, DON'T FORGET TO SHAMPOO **AND** CONDITION YOUR HAIR!!

WHOOSH

HMPH! YOU'RE FREE TO MOVE AROUND NOW.
ONCE WE'RE OUT OF THE ATMOSPHERE, IT'S QUIET.
HUH?! A-ALREADY ?!

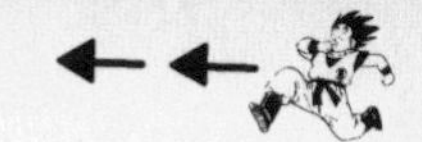

I WANTED TO SEE EARTH.
HEY, WHERE ARE YOU GOING, BULMA...?

LEAVE ME ALONE, I'M GOING TO CHANGE!

HUH? CHANGE... INTO YOUR PAJAMAS? YOU'RE GOING TO SLEEP ALREADY?

SLAM

BY THE WAY, ARE YOU REALLY GOING TO STAY
IN THOSE SUNDAY-SCHOOL CLOTHES THIS WHOLE TIME?

HEH HEH...
THIS...

OH SHOOT... COME TO THINK OF IT, I FORGOT MY PAJAMAS... WHAT ABOUT YOU, GOHAN?
I BROUGHT MINE.
NO, ACTUALLY, I MADE SOME CLOTHES WITHOUT TELLING MOM...

YOU MUST REALLY RESPECT PICCOLO...
YES! ABOUT THE SAME AS DAD.

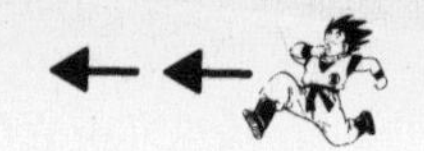

TUMP

HUH...? WH-WHAT STRANGE PAJAMAS...
THEY LOOK UNCOM-FORTABLE TO SLEEP IN...

OF COURSE THEY'RE NOT PAJAMAS !!
LOOKING AT YOU, I STARTED TO FEEL RIDICULOUS FOR HAVING SO ENTHUSIASTICALLY PREPARED FOR OUTER SPACE!
HO HO HO!!

S- SAY...
DID WE DO SOME-THING WRONG... ?
KURIRIN
I-I DON'T KNOW...

AND SO THE 3 TOOK OFF TO PLANET NAMEK...
NOT KNOWING THE TERROR THAT AWAITED THEM...

NEXT: Vegeta Returns!

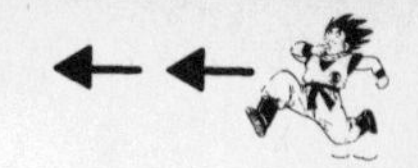

DBZ : 52 • The Return of Vegeta

IT MUST BE THERE!
SEEKING THE NEW DRAGON BALLS, BULMA, KURIRIN, AND SON GOHAN SET OUT TO PLANET NAMEK, THE HOME OF PICCOLO AND KAMI-SAMA. HOWEVER...

I'M BORED TO DEATH...
SIGH...
FASHION
ORANGE

YAWWN...

OH GEEZ... IT'S STILL ONLY THE 7TH DAY... 20-PLUS DAYS TO GO...
I SHOULD'VE MADE SOME STASIS CHAMBERS OR SOMETHING.
ARE YOU GUYS IMAGE-TRAINING AGAIN...?
YOU'RE LUCKY YOU CAN KILL TIME LIKE THAT...

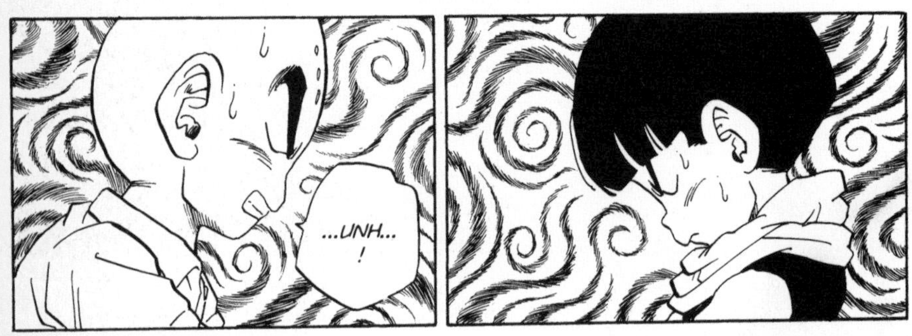
...UNH... !

HUFF HUFF...
AH !

YOU'RE GOOD! YOU REALLY ARE STRONG.
AFTER ALL, YOU'RE DESCENDED FROM GOKU AND YOU WERE TRAINED BY PICCOLO...
BUT I WAS SURPRISED AT THE NUMBER OF MOVES YOU HAVE!

SAY, TRAINING IN YOUR MIND IS ALL WELL AND GOOD...
...BUT THIS PLACE HAS GOTTEN PRETTY MESSY, SO COULD YOU CLEAN IT UP?
THERE'S A LADY IN HERE!

B-BUT YOU'RE THE ONE WHO MADE THE MESS OVER THERE...
WE CLEANED UP OUR OWN TRASH ALREADY...

I'M BUSY! THERE'S LOTS OF STUFF I HAVE TO THINK ABOUT.
ALL YOU GUYS HAVE TO DO IS JUST SIT ON BOARD.

I THOUGHT YOU SAID YOU WERE BORED...
SHUT UP! CAN'T YOU BE CON-SIDERATE TO A DELICATE LADY...?

BUSY BUSY!
...
IF SHE'S A LADY, I WISH SHE WOULDN'T WANDER AROUND IN HER UNDER-WEAR...

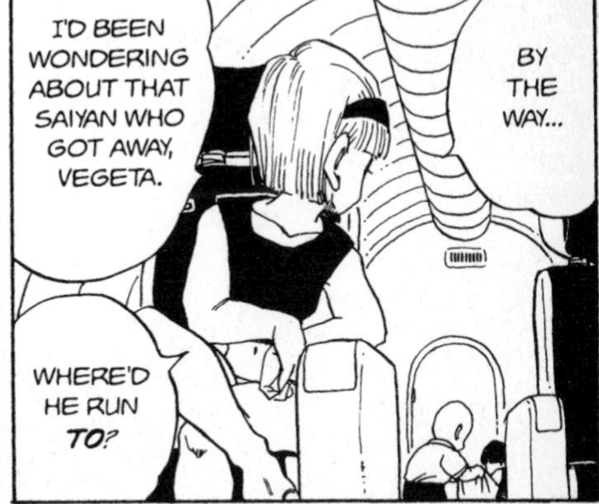
BY THE WAY...
I'D BEEN WONDERING ABOUT THAT SAIYAN WHO GOT AWAY, VEGETA.
WHERE'D HE RUN *TO*?

HUH? WHERE...?
I MEAN, THEIR PLANET'S LONG GONE, RIGHT?

I WONDER IF HE'S GETTING TREATED BY THOSE ALIENS...
HMM... SON-KUN'S BROTHER SAID ONCE... "WE LOCATE HOSPITABLE PLANETS AND SELL THEM TO OTHER RACES LOOKING FOR LIVING SPACE."

SO I'D THINK IT WOULD BE SOME PLANET WITH CIVILIZATION...
...OH YEAH... IN ANY CASE, HE ALSO TOOK A LOT OF DAMAGE...

...EARTH HAS SURE GOTTEN MARKED BY AN UNBE-LIEVABLE GUY...

IF THAT'S THE CASE, HOW SOON HE COMES BACK TO EARTH WOULD DEPEND ON WHERE THAT PLANET IS...
WE'D HAVE MORE TIME IF IT WERE FAR AWAY...

BULMA'S CONJECTURES WERE NOT WRONG AT ALL...
WHOOO

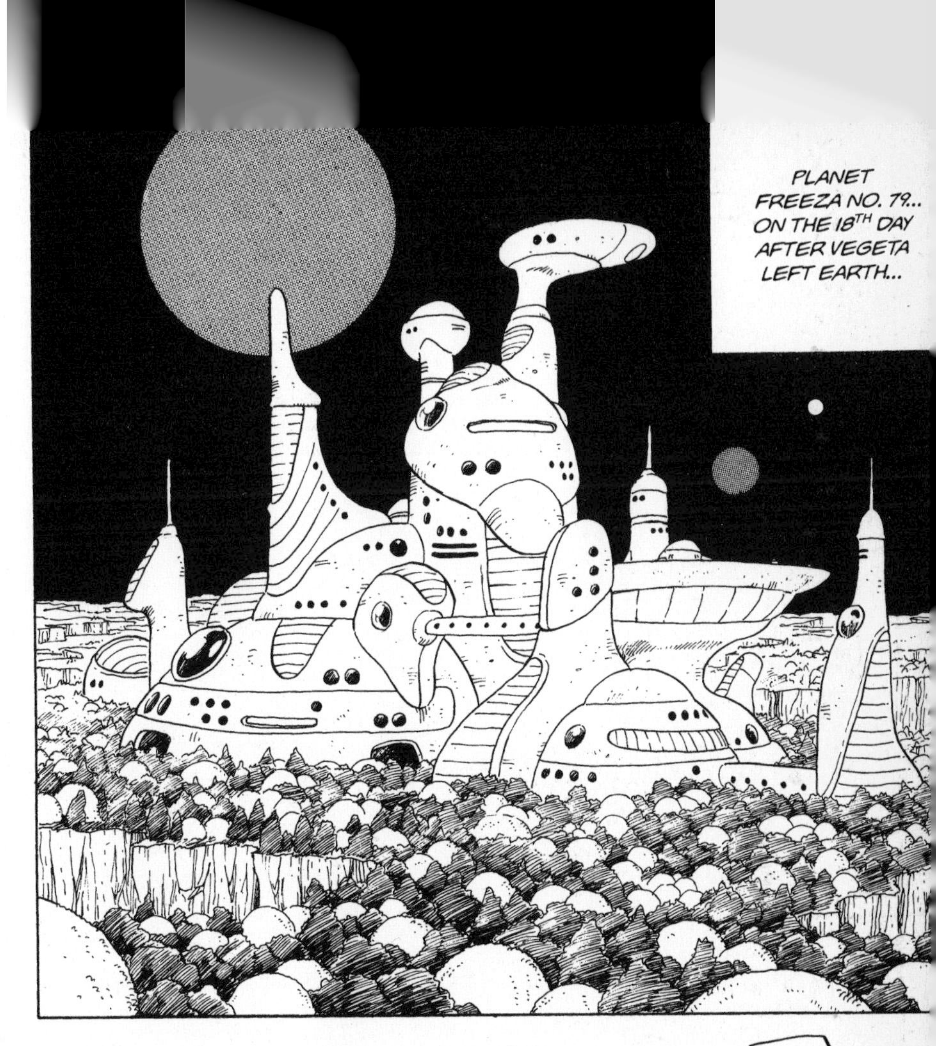
PLANET
FREEZA NO. 79...
ON THE 18TH DAY
AFTER VEGETA
LEFT EARTH...

pii
pii
HM
?
SOME-
THING'S
COMING
!

IS IT LORD FREEZA?!
IT COULDN'T BE!! HE JUST WENT OUT!

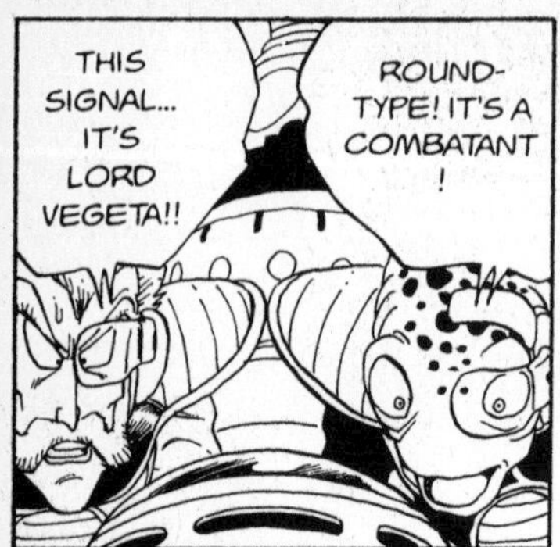
ROUND-TYPE! IT'S A COMBATANT!
THIS SIGNAL... IT'S LORD VEGETA!!

ODD! WE HADN'T BEEN INFORMED OF HIS RETURN!
DID SOMETHING HAPPEN?!
HEY!! THIS IS CONTROL!! LORD VEGETA IS ARRIVING!! SOMEONE RECEIVE HIM AT ONCE!!

HYEEEE

HYEEEEE
HERE HE COMES !!!
IT *IS* JUST ONE POD. WHERE'S NAPPA?!

WHAM

Ten-HUT!

...?

WH-WHAT'S THE MATTER...?! HE'S NOT COMING OUT...
H-HEY, HIS LIFE SIGNS ARE AWFULLY WEAK!!

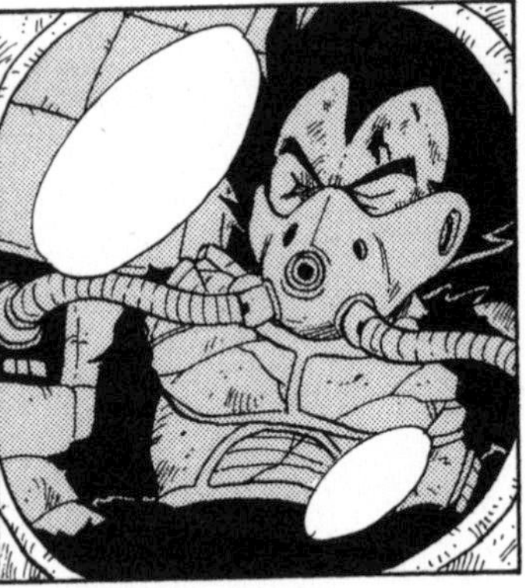

HE'S USING LIFE SUP-PORT!!
TH-THIS IS BAD!! TAKE HIM TO THE TREATMENT CENTER, NOW!!!

BLUP
BLOOP
ALL
RIGHT.

GLUG
GLUG

SHHK

WHIIIIIIU
YOU'RE ALL
HEALED. YOU
MAY OPEN
YOUR EYES
NOW.

UNFORTUNATELY,
YOUR TAIL COULD
NOT BE
REGENERATED...
NO
MATTER,
IT'LL GROW
BACK
AGAIN.

YOU MUST'VE HAD A HARD TIME EVEN WITH YOUR GREAT STRENGTH... TO THINK THAT THIS SUPER QUALITY RUBBER ARMOR WAS DESTROYED...

IS LORD FREEZA IN?
NO, HE HAS GONE OUT...

LORD KIWI SAID FOR YOU TO COME TO THE TRAINING ROOM AFTER YOUR TREATMENT, AS HE HAD TO TALK TO YOU...
HAH!
TELL HIM THAT I HAVE NOTHING TO SAY TO HIM.

HMPH...!
HE'S TIRED OF THIS PLANET ALREADY...

OH...! YOU FORGOT YOUR SCOUTER...

I DON'T NEED IT. IT'S YOURS.
WHAT?

I'LL HEAD TO EARTH FIRST THING TOMORROW MORNING... !
I'LL DESTROY THEM THIS TIME FOR SURE... !
NO... I SHOULD GO TO PLANET NAMEK FIRST...

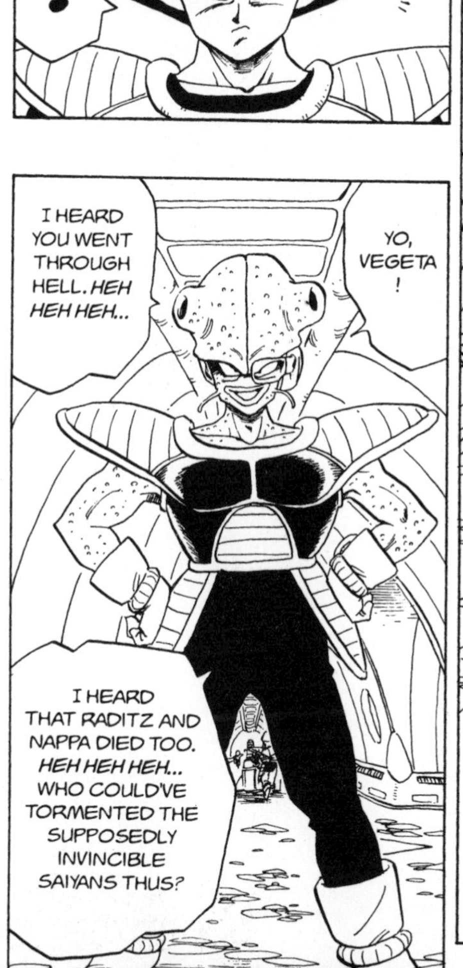
!
YO, VEGETA !
I HEARD YOU WENT THROUGH HELL. *HEH HEH HEH...*
I HEARD THAT RADITZ AND NAPPA DIED TOO. *HEH HEH HEH...* WHO COULD'VE TORMENTED THE SUPPOSEDLY INVINCIBLE SAIYANS THUS?

LORD FREEZA IS ANGRY THAT YOU GUYS DID ALL THIS WITHOUT HIS PERMISSION.
HMPH. HE CAN'T COMPLAIN IF HE'S NOT HERE.
NOW, LISTEN!
GRIP
I DON'T HAVE THE TIME TO WASTE LISTENING TO YOUR BLATHER.
GET THE HELL OUT OF MY FACE, KIWI.

NOW GET YOUR DIRTY HAND OFF ME.
BUT LORD FREEZA IS A GENEROUS PERSON.
I HEAR HE'S GOING TO FORGIVE YOU SINCE YOU DISCOVERED SOMETHING WONDERFUL...
WHAT ?!

HE WAS VERY PLEASED
THAT HE MIGHT OBTAIN ETERNAL YOUTH AND LIFE.
WHAT ?!
THEN LORD FREEZA HAS TAKEN OFF TO...!!
PLANET NAMEK !

DAMMIT! HE LISTENED TO OUR CONVERSATION THROUGH THE SCOUTERS... I SHOULD'VE KNOWN BETTER...!
I-I HAVE TO BEAT HIM THERE, OR I'LL HAVE TO DO HIS BIDDING FOREVER... !!

I HEAR THAT YOU HAD WANTED ETERNAL LIFE WITH THESE DRAGON BALLS TOO, BUT GIVE IT UP. *HA HA HA* !
LORD FREEZA IS PLANNING TO ANNIHILATE THE NAMEKIANS ONCE HE GETS HIS WISH.
UNH... !

THAT BAS-TARD... !!
DASH
HEY, VEGETA !!

WHOOSH
VEGETA !!

HE'S NOT GOING TO GET AWAY WITH THAT...!!
THOSE DRAGON BALLS ARE MINE!!!

AND ON THE 34TH DAY AFTER LEAVING EARTH... BULMA AND CO. FINALLY ARRIVED AT THEIR DESTINATION, PLANET NAMEK...
WE DID IT!!! THERE IT IS!!

NEXT: Planetfall

DRAGON BALL

ドラゴンボール

DBZ : 53

Planet Namek, Cold and Dark

KAMESEN
KULILIN

UN-BELIEV-ABLE !!
SO THAT'S PLANET NAMEK !
WOW! IT'S PRETTY !

FASTEN YOUR SEATBELTS, WE'RE IN FOR A BUMPY LANDING!
OKAY !

THAT'S **IF** WE CAN FIND A PLACE TO LAND AT ALL.....!
Piiii

HYUUUUUUN
WHOA !!

BOOM

YEEP !!
WE DID IT!! WE'VE LANDED ON PLANET NAMEK!!
WOW !!

HANG ON...
I'LL CHECK THE ATMO-SPHERIC COMPO-SITION.
LUCKILY I WAS SMART ENOUGH TO ATTACH EXTER-NAL SENSORS!

NOW, IF THERE'S JUST ANY AMOUNT OF OXYGEN...
piip piip
I BROUGHT OXYGEN MASKS JUST IN CASE, BUT OUR TIME OUTSIDE'D BE AWFULLY LIMITED....

THIS... LOOKS A LITTLE LIKE THE PLACE WHERE PICCOLO TRAINED ME...
YEAH... THE PLACE WHERE WE FIRST FOUGHT THE SAIYANS, RIGHT? PIC PROB'LY INSTINCTIVELY FELT BETTER IN A PLACE THAT LOOKED LIKE "HOME"...

OH, YEAH, WHY DON'T YOU FELLOWS JUST STROLL ON OUT?! DID YOU BRING LAWN CHAIRS?!!!
KURIRIN

HUH? WHAT'S SHE MAD ABOUT THIS TIME ?!
I-I DON'T KNOW...
MAYBE SHE'S JEALOUS 'CAUSE WE GOT OFF FIRST...
KURIRIN

SHEESH...!! LET'S JUST START LOOKING FOR THE DRAGON BALLS!!!
CHK CHK

!?

Piiii

LOOK!!!
WE HAVE A READING...!! THERE ***ARE*** DRAGON BALLS HERE!!!
YOU'RE RIGHT !!!!

WE DID IT! WE DID IT! WOO HOO!!

KURIRIN...
THERE'S SOME STRONG ***CHI*** THAT WAY...
CHI ?

...
Y- YOU'RE RIGHT... !!
KAMESEN KURIRIN

I FEEL A LOT OF THEM...
Y- YEAH...
AND EVERY ONE OF 'EM'S STRONG...

WH- WHAT COULD IT BE... ?

DUH! WHAT DO YOU EXPECT? THOSE ARE NAMEKIANS!
IF KAMI-SAMA AND PICCOLO WERE AS STRONG AS THEY WERE, THEN OF COURSE ***REAL*** NAMEKIANS ARE GONNA HAVE AMAZING CHI-POWER!

B-BUT... THEY'RE...
YEAH... EVIL, THAT'S WHAT THEY ARE....

OH, COME ON! THE LORD OF WORLDS HIMSELF SAID THE NAMEKIANS ARE GENTLE AND PEACEFUL AND...
AND LOOK! ISN'T THAT EXACTLY WHERE THE RADAR'S SHOWING FOUR BALLS GROUPED TOGETHER?

KAMESEN
KURIRIN
Y-YEAH! OF...OF COURSE!
IT'S ONLY THE NAMEKIANS!

SO LET'S GO MEET THESE NAMEKIANS!
HA! YOU GUYS'LL WORRY ABOUT ANY-THING!

HA HA...
KIII—IIN

HUH ?!

KIII—IIN

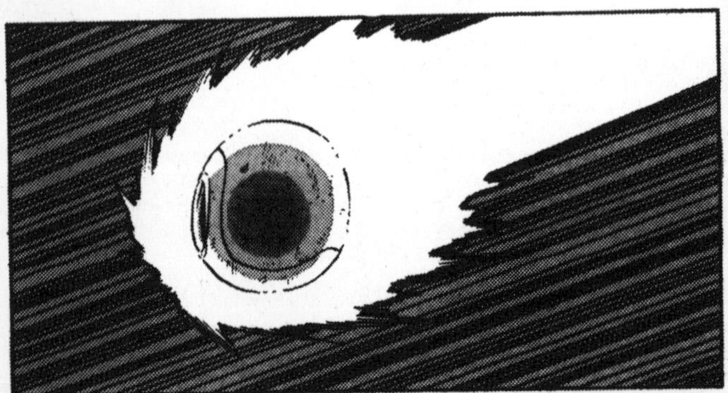

D-DOES THAT LOOK... KINDA F-FAMILIAR... ?

KIII——IIN
IT'S THE SAIYAN'S SPACESHIP !!!!

N-N-NO !!!

DOOM

H-H-HOW CAN THAT BE...?
IT CAN'T BE!! CAN IT?! BUT IT *IS* !!!!
...!!

GOHAN!!! SUPPRESS YOUR CHI!!! HE'LL SENSE YOU!!!
R-RIGHT !!!

IT'S VEGETA...! IT HAS TO BE... !!
I CAN'T BELIEVE THIS...! WHY WOULD... ?!

FUMP
DID THE SAIYAN... G-GET HEALED ALREADY... ?
DON'T YOU REMEMBER? HE WAS LOOKING FOR THE DRAGON BALLS TOO!
PWAP

WH-WH-WHAT ARE WE GOING TO DO... ?!
NO!! I KNOW WHAT WE'RE GOING TO DO!! WE'RE GOING BACK TO EARTH!! NOW!!!

BUT IF HE GETS AHOLD OF THOSE DRAGON BALLS...
BULMA, YOU GO BACK TO EARTH BY YOURSELF....

WE'LL STAY-- AND WE'LL GET THOSE DRAGON BALLS!
IT'LL BE ALL RIGHT... WE HAVE THE DRAGON RADAR...

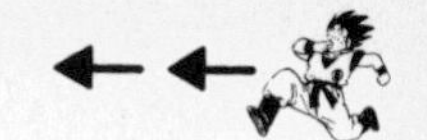

...RIGHT, GOHAN...?
Y-YEAH!!!

OKAY! FIRST I'LL SEND A WARNING TO THE TURTLE HERMIT....
ONCE I REACH EARTH, I'LL GRAB GOKU AND COME BACK! IT'LL BE A LITTLE OVER TWO MONTHS ROUND TRIP... WAIT FOR US!

T-TWO MONTHS... RIGHT....

THAT STINKING FREEZA...
THE DRAGON BALLS... ARE MINE...!!

THEY MUST HAVE LEARNED ABOUT MY REBELLION BY NOW...FREEZA WILL WANT ME DEAD...
I FEAR NO ONE ELSE...BUT FREEZA IS ANOTHER MATTER...
I'LL HAVE TO TAKE THE DRAGON BALLS SOMEHOW... AND ATTAIN IMMORTALITY.

HMPH...
I DIDN'T THINK I'D HAVE TO USE THE SCOUTERS AGAIN...
Piii

pi pi pi!

THIS WAY !
HE'S BROUGHT ZARBON AND DODORIA WITH HIM AS WELL... !!

KAME HOUSE

Y-YOU SAW **WHO** ?!
HE WHAT...?!
...UH-HUH... UH-HUH...

GOT IT?! NOW TELL THAT TO GOKU! AND EVERYBODY!
EXCEPT... WHATEVER YOU DO, DON'T TELL CHI-CHI!

THANKS! BYE!
HM?

HUH?!
H-HOW COULD THAT...!!
HUH? WHAT...?!

KIII~IIN

...
H-HEY...

WH-WH-WHAT'S THAT THING DOING...?!
TH-THAT'S WHAT WE'D LIKE TO KNOW...
DOOOM

IT IS OURS, LORD FREEZA !!

THANK YOU.
NOW WE HAVE THREE LEFT TO GO.

LOOK AFTER IT WELL, DEAR DODORIA.
I HEAR THAT VEGETA IS AFTER THEM...
YES, SIR!

LORD FREEZA, KIWI HAS ARRIVED JUST NOW, PURSUING VEGETA. THE TWO LARGE POWER READINGS THAT SUDDENLY APPEARED AND DISAPPEARED HAVEN'T YET RETURNED.
WE'RE IN-VESTIGATING THE AREA OF THE READINGS. WITH LUCK, WE'LL SOON KNOW WHAT THEY WERE.

FINE, FINE. BUT OUR PRIORITY IS THE REBELLIOUS VEGETA.
KIWI WILL DISPATCH HIM SOON ENOUGH. THOSE TWO ALWAYS DID HATE EACH OTHER.

THEIR ABILITIES ARE BASICALLY EQUAL, WHICH SHOULD AT LEAST STOP VEGETA FROM TAKING THE DRAGON BALL!

YOU WON'T GET AWAY, VEGETA !
I'LL SEE TO THAT MYSELF... !

NEXT: The Wecoming Party!

DBZ : 54 • The Mysterious Strangers

O--KAY... SO HOW DO WE GET OUT OF **THIS** MESS?!!
TH- THERE SHOULDN'T BE ANY MORE SAIYANS... WHO **WAS** THAT...?!

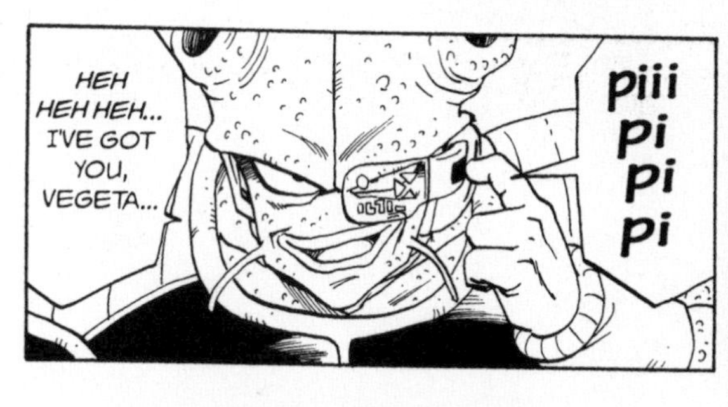

piii pi pi pi
HEH HEH HEH... I'VE GOT YOU, VEGETA...

AND THE ORDERS I'VE WANTED FROM LORD FREEZA !!
DO YOU HEAR ME, VEGETA?! AT LAST I CAN KILL YOU !!!!
HWAH!

DON'T MAKE ME LAUGH, KIWI.
DO YOU REALLY THINK YOU CAN KILL ME?
I'LL WAIT FOR YOU. DON'T DAWDLE.

HAAH HA HA! ARE YOU BLIND?! LOOK AT YOUR SCOUTER!!
MY COMBAT POWER IS WELL ABOVE YOURS!

HEH!..

WELL THEN...I'M OFF TO EARTH!! GOOD LUCK!!
I'LL BE RIGHT BACK-- IN TWO MONTHS!!

BULMA... WAIT A MINUTE...!!

G-GOHAN, WH-WHAT SHOULD WE DO ...?
M-MAYBE WE SHOULD GO BACK TO EARTH TOO, FOR A WHILE?
HUH?

I-IT L-LOOKS LIKE THERE'S MORE THAN ONE ENEMY...
I-I MEAN, I'M FINE, N-NO PROBLEM...BUT IF ANYTHING BAD HAPPENED TO Y-YOU.... !!

BUT THEN... WOULDN'T HE GET THE DRAGON BALLS...?
W-WELL, YEAH... F-FOR NOW! THEN WHEN WE COME B-BACK WE CAN TAKE 'IM ON AGAIN AN'--

IF SHENLONG DOESN'T GET KILLED FIRST, LIKE LAST TIME WITH PICCOLO...

...
...BUT...
!?

KURIRIN, SOMEONE'S COMING !!
HUH ?!

I-IS IT A SAIYAN ?!
NO... IT'S NOT VEGETA... IT'S A MUCH WEAKER **CHI**...

IT SHOULD BE AROUND HERE THAT THE READING BROKE OFF...
PROBABLY JUST A NAMEKIAN....

GULP...
IT'S PR- PROBABLY A NAMEKIAN...

HUH ?!
WHAT IS THAT?!

HUH ?!
TH- THEY'RE NOT NAMEKIANS !!!

THEY DON'T LOOK NAMEKIAN. WHO ARE THEY?
HEH HEH HEH, IT DOESN'T MATTER.
OUR ORDERS ARE TO KILL EVERYONE ON THIS PLANET...

L-LOOK AT THEIR CLOTHES... THEY'RE THE SAME AS WHAT THE SAIYANS WERE WEARING...
...BUT THEY'RE NOT SAIYANS...

I-I DUNNO WHAT'S GOING ON... BUT I GOT A BAD FEELING...

Y- Y- YEAH...
WHATEVER THEY'RE WEARING... THEY DON'T LOOK LIKE THEY WANT TO MAKE FRIENDS...!

FWOOO

GOHAN--
SUPPRESS YOUR CHI AND CONCENTRATE IT!
O-
OKAY.

pi
pi
pi
HA! DID YOU SEE THAT? THEY HAVE PRACTICALLY NO COMBAT POWER. THEY MUST BE TOURISTS!
HEH HEH HEH... IT'LL BE NO FUN IF THEY RUN. DO THE SPACESHIP FIRST.

ALL RIGHT
!
!?
!?

ZIII

BOOM
EEK !!!

GACK!!!!

TH- THE SPACE- SHIP !!!
SSSS...

HAAH HA HA!!
YIP...!
BAD LUCK, LITTLE TOURISTS!! YOU SHOULD HAVE COME LAST WEEK!!

GOHAN-- THESE GUYS ARE NOTHING!
RELEASE YOUR CHI!

HEY, DID YOU HEAR THAT?
HA HA HA! YEAH, WE'RE "NOTHING"-- JUST LIKE DEATH!

LET'S GO !!!

YEAH !!!

ZWOOOM

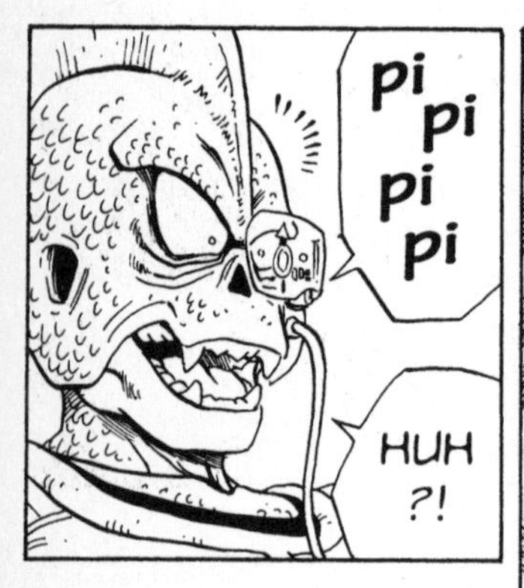
pi pi pi pi
HUH ?!

WH- WHAT IS THIS... ?!
TH-THIS POWER LEVEL-- IT'S TOO HIGH!!

SHHP

SHHP

NO--
!!

FP
FP

KRAK
WMM

YAAA
!!!!
WAK

HWRRRRR

BLOOSH
BLOOSH
TP
TP

PHEW.
HEY!
THAT WAS NICE!
IT WAS NOT!!!

Piiii

WHAT IS THE TROUBLE, LOYAL ZARBON?

LORD FREEZA... CONCERNING THE RECON-NAISSANCE WE SENT OUT EARLIER...
IT APPEARS WE'RE FACING MORE THAN ORDINARY BEINGS. THEIR POWER INDICES ROSE SHARPLY FOR A MOMENT, AND AFTER DEFEATING OUR SCOUTS, DISAPPEARED AGAIN...
I SEE.

THAT IS ODD. IT DOES NOT SOUND LIKE VEGETA...
THE READING IS QUITE DIFFERENT FROM VEGETA'S.

THEIR POWERS WERE BOTH ABOUT 1500.

1500...
I WOULD LIKE TO LEARN MORE ABOUT THEM, BUT CIRCUMSTANCES DO NOT GIVE US THE LUXURY.
IF YOU FIND THEM AGAIN, ELIMINATE THEM.

IT'S...IT'S NO USE... IT'S ALL OVER...
WE CAN NEVER GET BACK TO EARTH!
hic SOB

B-BULMA... W-WE'RE IN DANGER HERE....
THERE M-MIGHT BE STRONGER GUYS C-COMING... WE GOTTA GO!

I GUESS THE *CHI* WE FELT WASN'T NAMEKIANS...IT WAS VEGETA'S PEOPLE...
WE CAN'T LET THEM FIND US...

W-WE GOTTA HIDE SOME-WHERE...
I'M SURE THE NAMEKIANS WILL FIX THE SHIP...
SIGH I WISH I HAD YOUR YOUTHFUL OPTIMISM...

HEH HEH HEH... SO, VEGETA...
IT APPEARS THE TIME HAS FINALLY COME FOR US TO SETTLE THE SCORE...

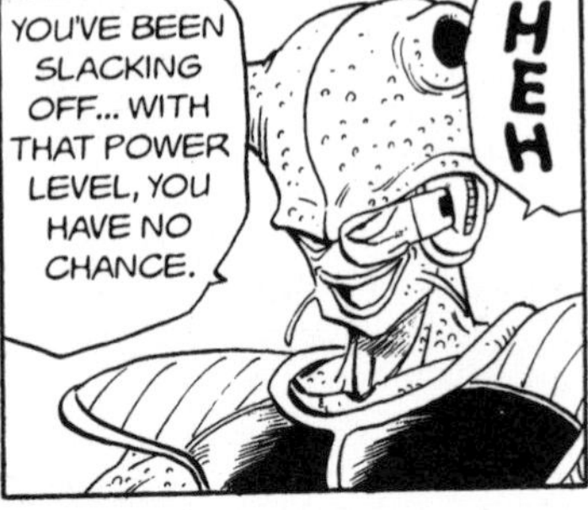
YOU'VE BEEN SLACKING OFF... WITH THAT POWER LEVEL, YOU HAVE NO CHANCE.
HEH

SOMETHING INTERESTING I LEARNED WHEN I WENT TO EARTH...
HAVEN'T I...? WELL THEN, I'LL HAVE TO SHOW YOU MY NEW DISCOVERY...

FEH!
HOW TO RUN AWAY QUICKLY?
NO. HOW TO CONCEAL MY TRUE POWER!!!!

NEXT: The True Power!

DBZ:55 • Vegeta's True Power!

YOU CAN... CONCEAL YOUR POWER LEVEL?!

RRRRG
WATCH MY COMBAT POWER NUMBER CLOSELY ON YOUR SCOUTER!!

pipipi..!!
I-IMPOSSIBLE...!!
Y-YOUR POWER...IS SUPPOSED TO BE THE SAME AS MINE...!!

FOOL!! I'VE BEEN FIGHTING CONTINUOUSLY-- IN REAL BATTLES!! ON EARTH I NEARLY DIED!!!
HOW CAN YOU KEEP UP WITH ME, SNUGGLING SAFE AND SOUND AT FREEZA'S?!

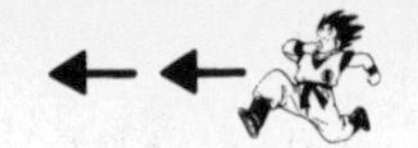

HYAAAAH...!!!!

19,000... 20,000...
pi pi pi
pi pi pi
21,000... 22,000... !!!!

BOOM

NNNKH...

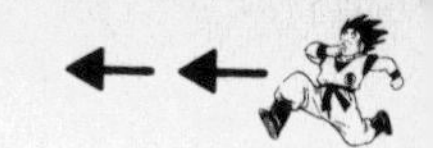

BOOM
!!

...
WHAT'S THE MATTER, ZARBON ?!

I-IT'S PROBABLY A MAL-FUNCTION..
BUT THE POWER-COUNTER SET TO VEGETA... J-JUST WENT PAST 22,000...!
TWUH... ?!

IT **HAS** TO BE A MALFUNCTION! YOUR SCOUTER'S A LEMON!
I'LL GET THE CORRECT NUMBER OFF MINE...

pipi pipi pi..!!

AND THE CORRECT NUMBER... ?
TH-THIS CAN'T BE RIGHT... I-I'VE GOT THE NEWEST SCOUTER ON THE MARKET! IT CAN'T BE **24,000**!!!

24,000?! THAT'S HIGHER THAN *OURS*!!
IT'S IMPOSSIBLE !!
VEGETA COULD BARELY GET UP TO 18,000!

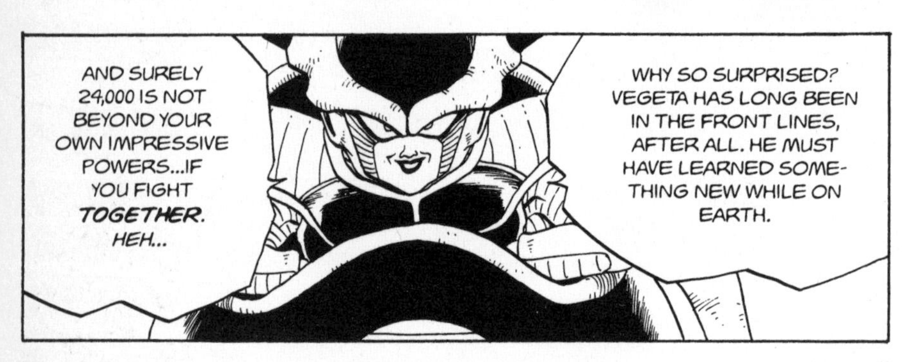
WHY SO SURPRISED? VEGETA HAS LONG BEEN IN THE FRONT LINES, AFTER ALL. HE MUST HAVE LEARNED SOME-THING NEW WHILE ON EARTH.
AND SURELY 24,000 IS NOT BEYOND YOUR OWN IMPRESSIVE POWERS...IF YOU FIGHT *TOGETHER*. HEH...

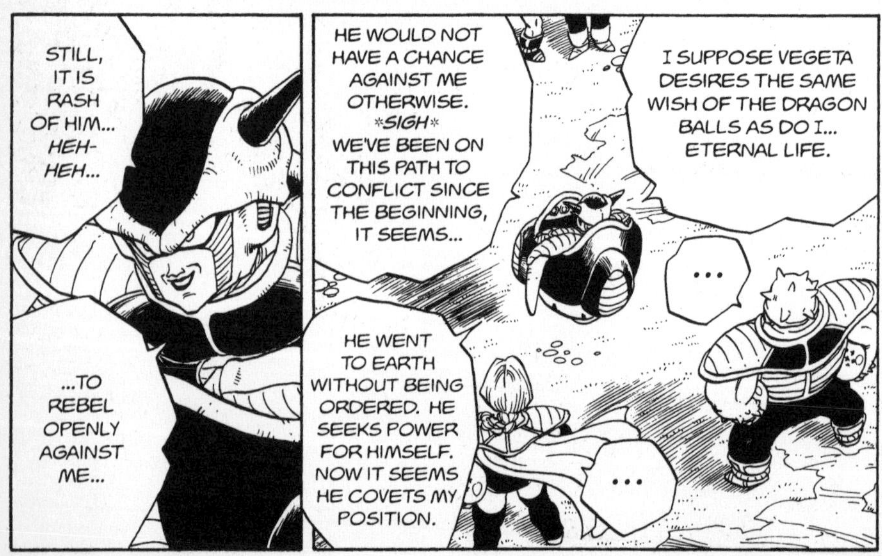
I SUPPOSE VEGETA DESIRES THE SAME WISH OF THE DRAGON BALLS AS DO I... ETERNAL LIFE.
...
...
HE WENT TO EARTH WITHOUT BEING ORDERED. HE SEEKS POWER FOR HIMSELF. NOW IT SEEMS HE COVETS MY POSITION.
HE WOULD NOT HAVE A CHANCE AGAINST ME OTHERWISE. *SIGH* WE'VE BEEN ON THIS PATH TO CONFLICT SINCE THE BEGINNING, IT SEEMS...
STILL, IT IS RASH OF HIM... HEH-HEH...
...TO REBEL OPENLY AGAINST ME...

W-WAIT, VEGETA! I JUST THOUGHT OF SOMETHING!
L-LET ME JOIN YOU!! HOW ABOUT IT?! I CAN HELP YOU OUT!!
I'VE SECRETLY HATED THE MAS--I MEAN, FREEZA--FOR A LONG TIME MYSELF!!

N-NOT BAD, EH?! WITH OUR POWERS COMBINED, WE COULD TAKE OUT ZARBON AND DODORIA LIKE NOTHING!

AND HERE I THOUGHT YOU WERE JUST A COWARD, KIWI...
BUT YOU'RE A LYING COWARD TOO!

...
LYING?! M-ME ?!

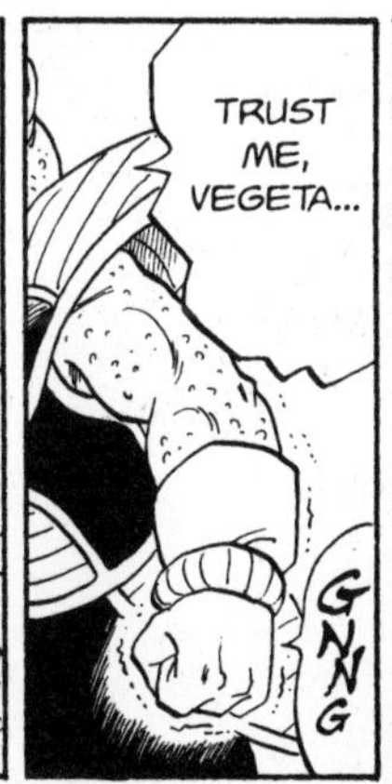
TRUST ME, VEGETA...
GNNG

OH!! MASTER FREEZA !!!
WHAT ?!

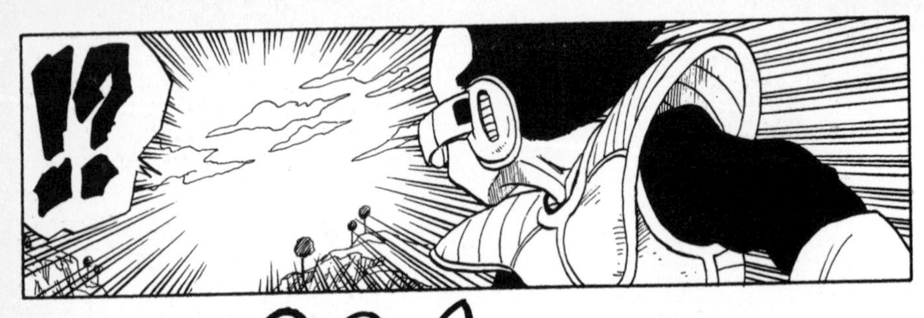
!?
!!

FOOL!!!!
WHOOSH

HYAAH!!!!
BADADADADADA...!!

SSHHHH!
HEH... HEH HEH HEH...

HA-HA-HA! BETTER A LIAR THAN A FOOL!
I DON'T CARE **HOW** STRONG YOU ARE--YOU'RE NOTHING IF YOU LEAVE YOURSELF WIDE OPEN!!

YOU DISAPPOINT ME, KIWI.
NOT YOUR ETHICS. BUT YOUR PATHETIC ATTEMPT AT **STRATEGY**.

B-B-BUT I JUST... !!!
IF MY POWER INCREASES... DOESN'T MY SPEED INCREASE ALONG WITH IT?
AND MY **RAGE**, KIWI. MY **RAGE** INCREASES WITH EACH OF YOUR STUPID ASSAULTS.

...

UNH
!!!
FWAA

IT'S
OVER,
KIWI
!!!!

V-N-N-N
VNNN

HOOOOSH
!!

KRII

DWOM

KRAK

HEH...

SHA

BOOM

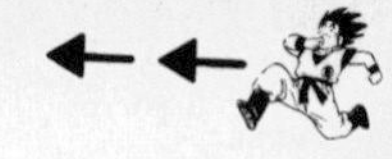

AH!
I'VE ALWAYS LOVED FIRE-WORKS!

TP

FREEZA'S MEN WILL BE FOLLOWING ME WITH THEIR SCOUTERS...
I CAN HANDLE ZARBON AND DODORIA, BUT IF I APPROACH TOO RECKLESSLY...
I'D HAVE NO CHANCE AGAINST FREEZA.

ACCORDING TO WHAT I OVERHEARD THROUGH THE SCOUTER, THE DRAGON BALLS HAVE NO EFFECT UNLESS YOU'VE GATHERED ALL SEVEN TOGETHER.
ALL RIGHT, THEN. I'LL FIND ONE OF THEM. ONCE THEY'VE FOUND THE OTHER SIX, I'LL LOOK FOR AN OPENING AND TAKE THEM FOR MYSELF.

IF THAT GOES WELL... ETERNAL LIFE WILL BE MINE...
AND DEFEATING FREEZA WILL NO LONGER BE A DREAM!

ONCE HE'S GONE, I WILL STAND SUPREME!!
VEGETA, THE SAIYAN, WILL RULE THE UNIVERSE!!!!

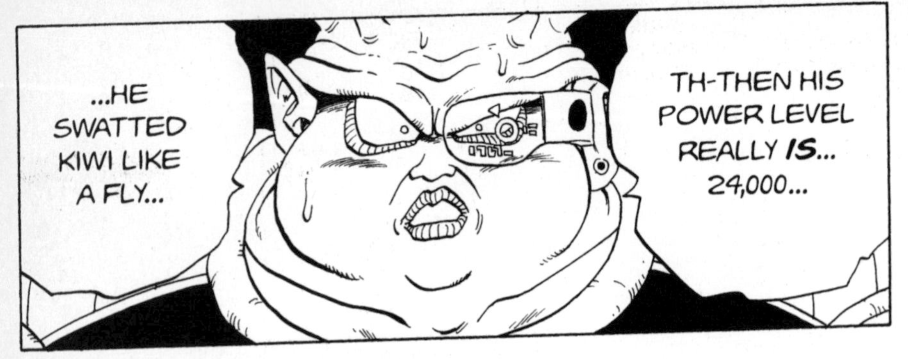
...HE SWATTED KIWI LIKE A FLY...
TH-THEN HIS POWER LEVEL REALLY ***IS***... 24,000...

I HAVE A READING OF TEN OR SO NAMEKIANS IN THAT DIRECTION.
EXCELLENT. LET'S HOPE THEY HAVE THE DRAGON BALL, MM?

THERE APPEAR TO BE OTHER STRANGE BEINGS OUT THERE...
IN THE MEANTIME, LET NONE OF US LET DOWN HIS GUARD.

NO MATTER.
LET US GO LOOK FOR THE FIFTH DRAGON BALL, SHALL WE?

LET US BE OFF!
YES, MASTER.

FMMM
FM

HOOOSH
HOOOSH

BULMA, CAN'T YOU GO ANY FASTER?! WE'RE SITTING DUCKS OUT HERE!
HUF PUF
YOU GUYS CAN FLY, CAN'T YOU?! SO CARRY ME!!

HEY! BULMA, LOOK OVER THERE!
WE'LL BE HARD TO SPOT IN THAT CAVE!

IT TAKES SO MUCH **CHI** TO FLY, THE BAD GUYS'D FIND US IF WE USED IT!
I WISH I COULD...BUT I CAN'T IF I'M GOING TO HIDE MY **CHI**...

SOB
hic
HUH?
KURIRIN... DO YOU FEEL SOME CHI THAT WAY?!
Y-YOU'RE RIGHT...!

B-BUT HOW LONG...
W-WILL WE HAVE TO ST-STAY THERE...?!
...

KAME SEN
KURIRIN
!!

THERE'S ANOTHER STRANGE CHI COMING RIGHT AT US!
HIDE!!!

FEELS DIFFERENT FROM THE GUYS WE RAN INTO EARLIER...
THEY COULD BE NAMEKIANS THIS TIME...

NEXT: Goku to the Rescue!... Sort of!

YOU TOO, BULMA-- HIDE!!! IT'S THE FRIENDS OF THE GUYS WE FOUGHT EARLIER!!!!
HUH ?!

Y'KNOW, I'VE BEEN MEANING TO ASK HOW YOU TWO CAN TELL THESE THINGS...
SHUT UP! THEY'RE COMING THIS WAY!

D-DO YOU TH-THINK THEY SPOTTED US...?
KURIRIN

KAMESEN KURIRIN

THEY'RE HERE !!

KIIIN
KIIIN

HYUUN
HYUUN
HYUUN

KIIIIIN

TH- THEY'RE GONE...
I GUESS WE WEREN'T WHAT THEY WERE AFTER!!

BUT... WHAT WERE THEY, ANYWAY?
THEY WENT BY SO FAST I COULDN'T SEE...

KURIRIN
BRRRR...

HUF
HUF
HUF

B-BULMA...? C-COULD YOU CONFIRM SOMETHING ON THE D-DRAGON RADAR...?
CONFIRM WHAT... ?
KURIRIN, WHAT'S WRONG... ?

TH-THERE WERE FOUR DRAGON BALLS... CL-CLUSTERED IN A GROUP... S-SEE IF THOSE GUYS WERE THE ONES WHO HAD 'EM...

CHK CHK

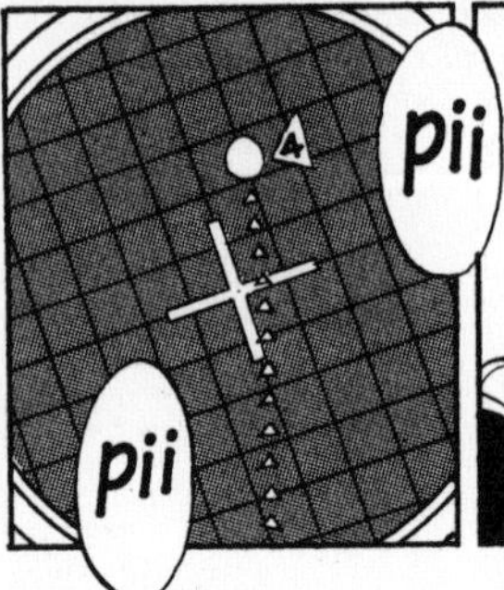
pii
4
pii

THEY WERE CARRYING FOUR DRAGON BALLS !!
YEAH!! NO DOUBT ABOUT IT!!

I KNEW IT...
KAMESEN KURIRIN

GOHAN... DID YOU SEE...? TH-THE WEIRD GUY FLYING SECOND FROM THE LEAD...
Y-YEAH...
I... SAW HIM...
...?

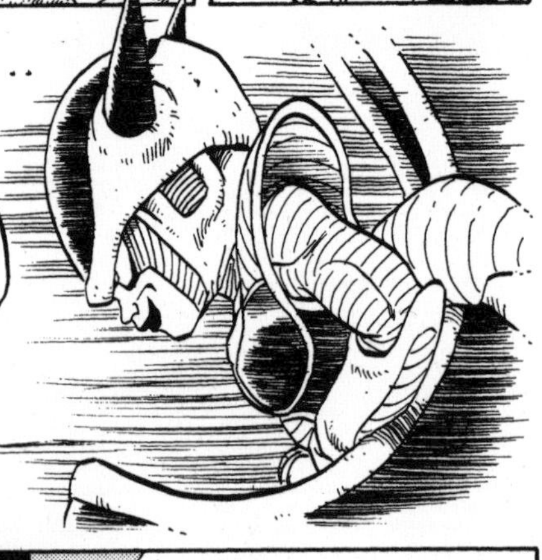

AND I FELT... HIS POWER...

KAMESEN KURIRIN
ME TOO. AND I *FROZE*. THAT LITTLE SQUIRT...COULD BE A LOT MORE POWERFUL THAN VEGETA...!

THE OTHERS WERE SOMETHIN', TOO... B-BUT ***HE***...!

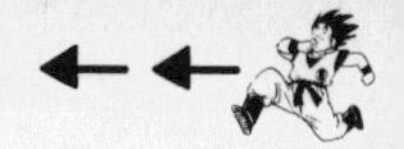

S-STRONGER... THAN VEGETA?! B-BUT WHO... WHO...?
I DON'T KNOW! B-BUT JUDGIN' BY THE CLOTHES, I'D SAY TH-THEY'RE ALL WITH VEGETA...

DAM-MIT...
HOW ARE WE S'POSED TO GET THE DRAGON BALLS AWAY FROM **THOSE** MONSTERS?

H-HEY!
LOOK...!
CHK CHK

THEY'RE HEADING STRAIGHT TOWARDS THIS **OTHER** DRAGON BALL...!

WHAT'S GOING ON?! DO THEY HAVE THEIR OWN RADAR...?
WH-WHERE IS THIS...?

ABOUT... 14KM IN THAT DIRECTION...

THAT'S WHERE WE FELT THE CHI YOU SAID MIGHT BE NAMEKIANS...
YEAH.

KAMESEN KURIRIN
I'M... G-GONNA GO THERE AND CHECK IT OUT...!

I'LL GO WITH YOU!

W-WAIT A MINUTE!! YOU'RE NOT GONNA LEAVE ME HERE ALL ALONE?!
I THINK IT'S A LOT SAFER HERE...

...
W-WELL... Y-YEAH...
OKAY. I'LL PUT UP A CAPSULE HOUSE INSIDE THE CAVE AND WAIT HERE.

THEN REPORT THIS TO MASTER MUTEN-RŌSHI, OKAY?

W-WILL DO. B-BE CAREFUL!
GOHAN, WE'VE GOTTA HURRY--BUT SUPPRESS OUR CHI AS MUCH AS WE CAN!
YOU THINK YOU CAN DO IT?
YEAH!

SHHHPP

SHH SHHAAA

MEANWHILE, IN THE HOSPITAL ON EARTH...
KONG HOSPITAL

NNNN!
UHHH!

NNKH!
RRRRG!
MMFF!

AHEM
NOT BEING RECKLESS AGAIN, ARE YOU, SON GOKU?

OH!
D-DOCTOR...
REALLY, NOW! HOW MANY TIMES DO I HAVE TO TELL YOU? IF YOU KEEP DOING THAT YOU'LL NEVER BE WELL ENOUGH TO BE DISCHARGED!

I DON'T BELIEVE YOUR NONSENSE ABOUT FIGHTING ALIENS...BUT FOR WHATEVER REASON, YOU'RE IN SERIOUS CONDITION.
S-SORRY...

WHERE'S YOUR WIFE?
SHOPPING. SAID SHE WAS BORED...

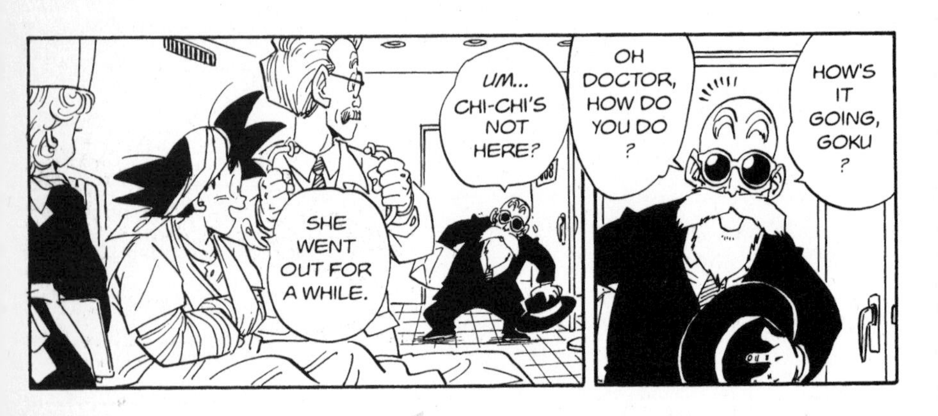
HOW'S IT GOING, GOKU?
OH DOCTOR, HOW DO YOU DO?
UM... CHI-CHI'S NOT HERE?
SHE WENT OUT FOR A WHILE.

PERFECT...
HERE'S SOME GET-WELL POUND CAKE FOR YOU. HAVE SOME.
THANKS!

GOKU... I RECEIVED WORD FROM BULMA ABOUT TWO HOURS AGO...
DID THEY GET TO PLANET NAMEK ALL RIGHT?
FONDLE FONDLE
EEEEK!

...
HM? DID I DO SOMETHING JUST NOW?
I MUST BE GETTING OLD. I DO THINGS WITHOUT REALIZING IT THESE DAYS...

YES, THEY REACHED NAMEK WITHOUT PROBLEMS...
UNFORTUNATELY...

THEY WEREN'T THE ONLY ONES WHO WENT TO THAT PLANET...
IT SEEMS THAT VEGETA... WENT THERE TOO...!

VEGETA ?!
BUT...
BUT THEN...

LISTEN TO ME. THE TURTLE JUST RADIOED ME... HE'S JUST RECEIVED NEW INFORMATION FROM BULMA, AND ACCORDING TO HIM...
...VEGETA HAS AT LEAST TEN COMRADES ON NAMEK. THEY DESTROYED OUR GROUP'S SPACESHIP... AND NOW THEY'RE STRANDED THERE!

WH- WHAT... ?!

AND... AT LEAST ONE OF THE TEN... HAS A CHI SURPASSING EVEN VEGETA'S...
...N- NO... NO !!

'EY, YO!
YOU ALIVE, MONKEY MAN?

WHAT? I THOUGHT YOU'D BE ALL HAPPY TO SEE ME!

SOME SENZU ARE FINALLY DONE. JUST A FEW THOUGH.
KARIN TOLD ME TO BRING YOU ALL SEVEN!

REALLY?! WHAT PERFECT TIMING!!
GIVE ME ONE! NOW!!

HERE YOU GO.
AAAH
H-HEY!! WHAT ARE YOU FEEDING TO MY PATIENT?!

MMF MMF

GLLLP

HEH

TM
UH ?!
FWA
BRRAK
I'VE BEEN WAITING FOR THIS MOMENT !!!
THE LORD OF WORLDS SENT THIS FROM HEAVEN...MY UNIFORM !!

ALL RIGHT !!
NAMEK, HERE I COME !!

THANKS, I'LL TAKE THE REST OF THEM!
T-TO PLANET NAMEK... B-BUT HOW?!

HEH HEH... WHEN BULMA'S DAD CAME TO SEE ME, I ASKED HIM...
...TO MAKE ME A SPACESHIP JUST IN CASE!

I SEE! THE SAME AS KAMI-SAMA'S?
NO, NO. THAT USED SOME ALIEN MATERIALS SO EVEN HE COULDN'T COPY IT.

TH-THEN...?

I THOUGHT REAL HARD...AND REMEMBERED THAT TWO SAIYAN SPACESHIPS HAD COME TO EARTH ***BEFORE*** VEGETA AND NAPPA!
THE ONE MY BROTHER CAME ON...
AND THE ONE ***I*** CAME ON WHEN I WAS A KID!

WITH THAT...
I CAN GET TO PLANET NAMEK IN 6 DAYS!

I HAD BULMA'S DAD GO LOOK FOR IT.
TH- THAT'S RIGHT !!
MY BROTHER'S HAD EXPLODED, BUT MINE WAS AN OLDER MODEL SO IT WAS SAFE! I HAD HIM FIX IT UP!

EEEEK !!!

WELL, I'M OFF TO SAVE 'EM!!
VWA

KINTO'UN !!!

TO BULMA'S HOUSE !!
HYUUUN
TP

SAVE... WHO?
W- WELL...
...HIS SON AND HIS TWO OLDEST FRIENDS...
...

WHAT?!
WHY'S HE LOOK SO **JAZZED** WHEN SOMETHING SO HORRIBLE IS HAPPENING ?!

I CAN ONLY THINK IT'S THE SAIYAN BLOOD...
HE DOES WANT TO SAVE THEM... BUT PART OF HIM JUST **LOVES** GOING UP AGAINST POWERFUL OPPONENTS...!

I DON'T KNOW WHETHER TO ADMIRE THE GUY OR PITY HIM...
I MEAN, HE'S OBVIOUSLY GOT NO CHANCE...

I CAN'T BELIEVE IT!
FIGHTERS EVEN STRONGER THAN VEGETA !

NEXT: Son Goku's Spaceship

ONE BEAN FROM MASTER KARIN'S "SENZU" PLANT... AND GOKU'S INJURIES WERE MAGICALLY HEALED.
NOW, HAVING LEARNED OF THE CRISIS THAT HIS SON AND FRIENDS ARE FACING ON PLANET NAMEK, GOKU RUSHES TO BULMA'S HOUSE TO FIND THE SAIYAN SPACESHIP THAT HE'D EARLIER WANTED RESTORED...JUST IN CASE...
CAPSULE CORP.

DBZ:57 • Son Goku's Spaceship

TMP
B1
HE'S GOT TO BE DONE!
HYUUN

WHERE WOULD HE HAVE IT...?
INSIDE THE HOUSE?

OH MY! IS THAT GOKU...?!
... BULMA'S MOM!

MY MY MY! YOU'RE LOOKING SO WELL!
GOOD AS NEW!

IS BULMA'S DAD DONE REBUILDING THAT SPACE-SHIP LIKE I ASKED...?
WELL...I THINK I SAW HIM STILL PUTTERING ON IT... MAYBE WE SHOULD TAKE A LOOK...

WHAT?!
Y-YOU MEAN HE HASN'T...?!

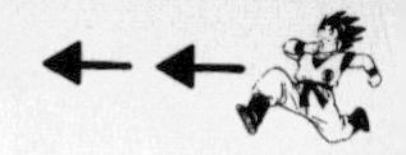

I CAN'T BELIEVE THAT PUNY LITTLE GOKU GREW UP TO BE SO **CHARMING**!
...
WE SHOULD GO OUT FOR DRINKS... AFTER YOU BEAT UP THOSE SAIYANS!

OH, BY THE WAY! I FOUND THIS **DELICIOUS** PASTRY SHOP THE OTHER DAY! AND IT'S ALL THANKS TO YOU! AFTER ALL, I WOULDN'T HAVE BEEN ABLE TO FIND IT IF EARTH HAD BEEN DESTROYED!
HA HA...

DEAR! LITTLE GOKU'S HERE!
HUH?

IS...
IS THIS IT?!

OH, HEY!
BETTER ALREADY, EH? THOSE SENZU SURE ARE SOMETHING!
THIS... THIS IS THE SPACE-SHIP?!
PSULE
CORP.
IT'S NOT FINISHED YET?!

OH, ALMOST, ALMOST...
COME ON IN AND TAKE A LOOK.
I'LL BRING SOMETHING TO DRINK. I'LL CALL PU'AR AND OOLONG OVER WHILE I'M AT IT.
UH... TH-THANKS.

WOW, IT'S HUGE!
HOW DID THAT TINY SPACESHIP GET SO BIG?
WHAT DO YOU THINK? EVERYTHING'S JUST LIKE YOU WANTED IT!

I COULD TRAIN ALL I WANT IN HERE.
I'VE BEEN WORKING HARD. HAD TO REBUILD ALMOST THE WHOLE THING.
THAT SAIYAN TECHNOLOGY SURE IS AMAZING.

WHAT ABOUT THE ARTIFICIAL GRAVITY GENERA-TOR?
OH, IT'S DONE. THIS IS IT.

THIS IS THE SWITCH FOR ARTIFICIAL GRAVITY... AND THIS IS THE CONTROLLER. IT USES THE SPACE-SHIP'S ACCELERATION. LIKE YOU ASKED, IT CAN GENERATE UP TO A MAXIMUM OF 100G...

BUT ISN'T THAT KIND OF EXTREME, EVEN FOR YOU? WITH 100G, IF YOU WEIGH 60 KG YOU BECOME **6000KG!** THAT'S ***6 TONS!***
PROBABLY KILL EVEN YOU.
IT'S OKAY. IF I COULDN'T HANDLE THAT MUCH I'D NEVER HAVE A CHANCE AGAINST THE SAIYAN.

BUT... CAN THIS THING FLY?
OH, IT CAN FLY. I'VE INPUT ALL THE DATA, SO ALL YOU HAVE TO DO IS PRESS THE SWITCH AND YOU'LL BE ON NAMEK IN SIX DAYS.

THE BATH, TOILET, KITCHEN, AND BEDROOM ARE DOWN THAT LADDER...
THEN... THEN WHAT ISN'T FINISHED... ?!

WELL, I CAN'T DECIDE WHERE TO PUT THE STEREO SPEAKERS...
I MEAN, YOU WANT TO HAVE GOOD SOUND, DON'T YOU?
TH-THAT'S IT?! THAT'S ALL THAT'S NOT FINISHED?!

"THAT'S ALL," HE SAYS!
POSITIONING SPEAKERS FOR THE BEST POSSIBLE SOUND IS AN ART FORM, I'LL HAVE YOU KNOW! WHEN YOU CONSIDER THE ACOUSTICS OF...

I DON'T CARE ABOUT THE STEREO!! I'M IN A HURRY!!
I'M GOING TO TAKE OFF RIGHT NOW!!!!

WHAT COULD BE SO IMPORTANT THAT YOU DON'T CARE ABOUT THE STEREO?
I GOT WORD FROM YOUR DAUGHTER--AND MY SON!! THEIR SPACESHIP HAS BEEN DESTROYED!! AND THE SAIYAN AND HIS GANG ARE ON NAMEK WITH THEM!!

MY GOODNESS...!
WELL, THAT IS URGENT, ISN'T IT?

TEACH ME HOW TO FLY THIS THING, NOW!!
ALL RIGHT! BUT YOU KNOW, ALL I NEED IS A FEW HOURS WITH THE SPEAKERS...

BWOOOOOOSH..
CAPSULE
CORP.

UM...
THIS ONE... !
BEEP!

URK !!!!!

NOT BAD CONSIDERING HOW FAST I THREW IT TOGETHER !
HMPH !

YEAH. HE WAS IN KIND OF A HURRY.
WAS THAT SOUND WHAT I THINK IT WAS...?
HUH?! WHERE'S GOKU?! WHERE'S THE SPACESHIP ?!

I WONDER IF SOMETHING HAPPENED...
I THOUGHT WE WERE FRIENDS... HE COULD'VE AT LEAST SAID HI.
HUH... ?

CAPSULE
DA-KOOOM

HWOOOO
CAPSULE

PHEW...! TH-THIS THING SURE IS FAST...!
BOY... OUTER SPACE IS DARK. IS IT NIGHT NOW...?

IT'S GREAT THAT I CAN GET THERE IN SIX DAYS...BUT THAT'S HARDLY LONG ENOUGH TO GET READY TO FIGHT VEGETA...
... DOESN'T MATTER. I BETTER START TRAINING !
VNN VNN

...LET'S SEE, I HEARD THE LORD OF WORLDS' PLACE HAD GRAVITY OF 10G...
I GUESS I SHOULD START GETTING USED TO 20G FOR NOW...
pi piiii
HOOOMF
OOG !!!

RRK !!
OHH... THAT'S... GRAVITY... !!
DOMP
DOMP

ONE TWO!
ONE TWO!

I'LL HAVE TO START RETRAINING FROM THE BASICS...
OR I'LL NEVER BE ABLE TO HANDLE THE MULTIPLE STRENGTH KAIŌ-KEN...!

WHOOSH
WHOOSH

WE'RE GETTING CLOSE!! SUPPRESS YOUR CHI COMPLETELY! WE'VE GOT TO SWITCH TO WALKING!
OK !!

I'M PICKING UP UNBELIEVABLE CHI...
GULP...

OVER THAT CLIFF... !

PEEK

HEY! TH-THERE ARE HOUSES... THAT LOOK LIKE OUR SPACE-SHIP...!
WH-WHAT ARE THEY DOING... ?!

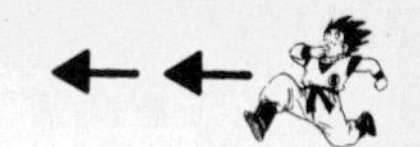

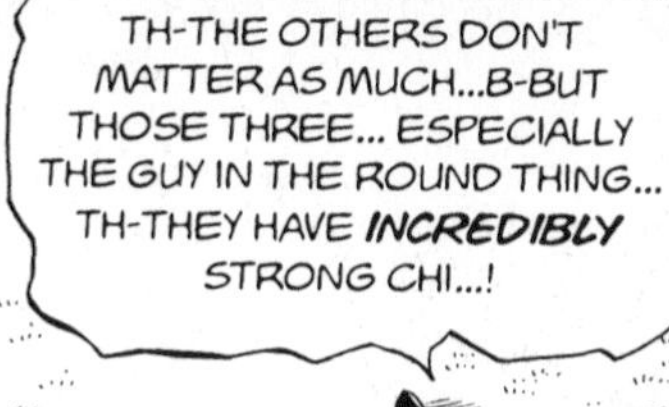
TH-THE OTHERS DON'T MATTER AS MUCH...B-BUT THOSE THREE... ESPECIALLY THE GUY IN THE ROUND THING... TH-THEY HAVE ***INCREDIBLY*** STRONG CHI...!

!!

HM ?

OH... !
L-LOOK AT WHAT THE TWO GUYS ON EACH SIDE ARE CARRYING...! D-DRAGON BALLS!
TH- THEY'RE HUGE... !

VSSH

WHAT IS THE MATTER, MR. DODORIA?
I DETECTED A VERY SMALL POWER READING IN THAT DIRECTION...
IT'S GONE NOW... IT MUST'VE BEEN A SMALL ANIMAL OR AN INSECT.

EESH... TH-THAT WAS CLOSE...!
PHEW...

MASTER FREEZA, WE FOUND ONLY FIVE OF THEM!
THE REST HAD JUST SLIPPED OUT!

OUTSIDE!! NOW--IF YOU DON'T WANT TO DIE!!

THEY LOOK JUST LIKE KAMI-SAMA AND PICCOLO...!! TH-THEY'RE NAMEKIANS...!!

NEXT: The Kindness of Freeza

DBZ : 58 • Namekian Fear

COME ON! STEP FORWARD!!
MOVE IT!!

WH-WHAT ARE THEY GOING TO DO WITH THOSE NAMEKIANS...?
K-KURIRIN... ARE THEY ALL SAIYANS?

NO... THEY HAVE THE SAME CLOTHES, BUT THEY'RE NOT SAIYANS...
BESIDES, THE ONLY SAIYAN LEFT SHOULD BE VEGETA...
...EXCEPT FOR YOU AND GOKU...

TH-THEN...
COME TO THINK OF IT, GOKU'S BROTHER SAID, "WE EXTERMINATE THE NATIVES OF HOSPITABLE PLANETS AND SELL THEM TO ALIENS"...
...MAYBE THEY'RE IN ON THAT TOO...

BUT IT DOESN'T LOOK LIKE VEGETA'S HERE... IS HE LOOKING FOR DRAGON BALLS SOME-WHERE ELSE...?!

!!
!!

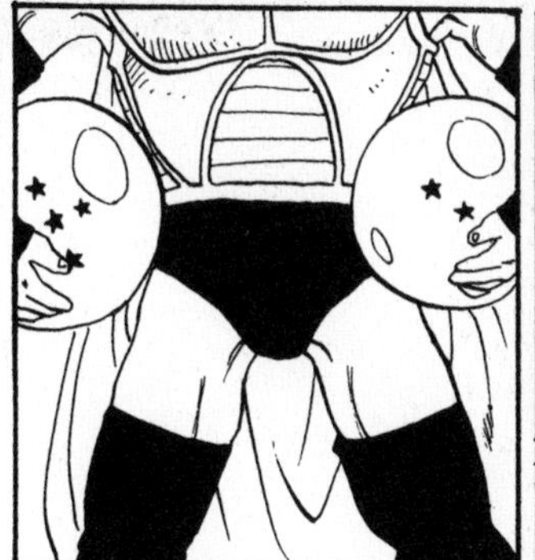

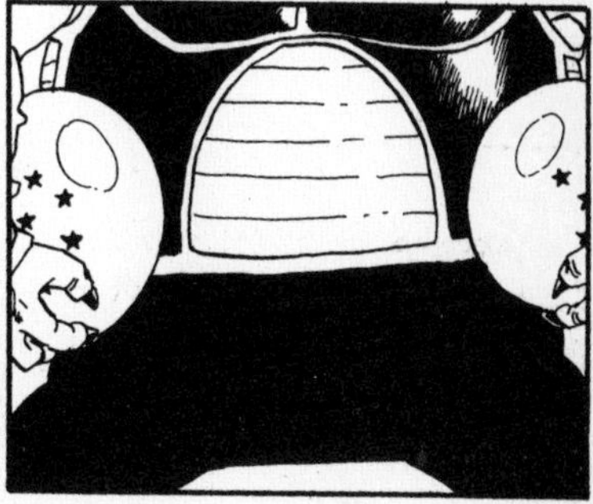

...
NNH...

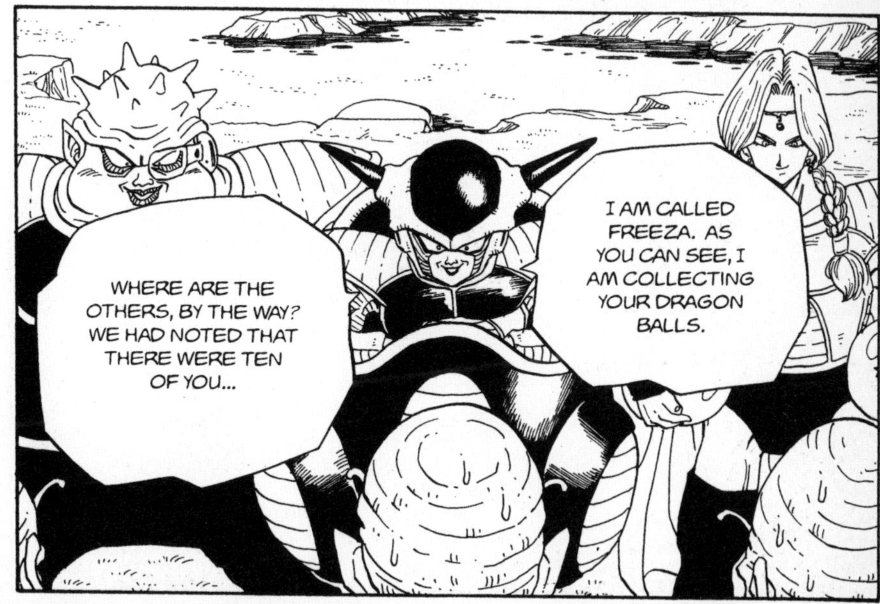
I AM CALLED FREEZA. AS YOU CAN SEE, I AM COLLECTING YOUR DRAGON BALLS.
WHERE ARE THE OTHERS, BY THE WAY? WE HAD NOTED THAT THERE WERE TEN OF YOU...

ARE YOU PLANNING TO REMAIN SILENT?
WE WILL HAVE TO KILL YOU.

...
!

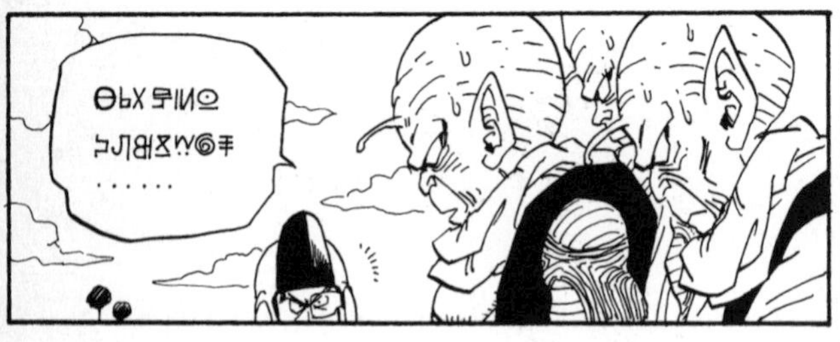
......

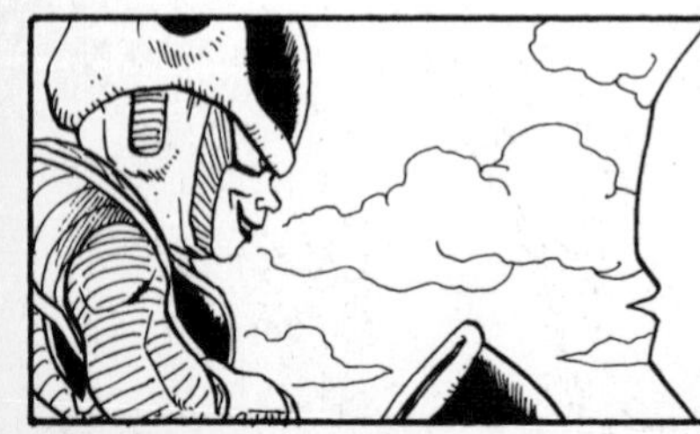
PLEASE SPEAK IN A TONGUE THAT WE UNDERSTAND, NOT NAMEKIAN. WE KNOW THAT YOU CAN SPEAK OUR LANGUAGE.

...
TH-THE OTHERS... WENT OUT TO WORK IN THE FIELDS... THE ONLY ONES HERE ARE THE ELDERLY AND THE CHILDREN...

THERE YOU GO. AS LONG AS YOU CAUSE NO TROUBLE AND ANSWER US, YOU WILL BE PERFECTLY FINE.

...

NOW. ON TO OTHER QUESTIONS.
WHERE IS THE DRAGON BALL? THERE IS ONE HERE, I'M QUITE SURE OF THAT.
I-I DON'T KNOW... I MEAN... WE DON'T HAVE ANYTHING LIKE THAT...!

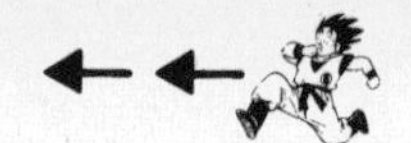

HEH
HEH
HEH...

MY DEAR DODORIA...IF I RECALL, THE SECOND NAMEKIAN WE KILLED SAID SOMETHING QUITE INTERESTING.
YES. SOMETHING TO THE EFFECT THAT THESE PEOPLE WILL ONLY HAND OVER THE DRAGON BALLS TO GREAT HEROES.

AH, YES. HE WAS VERY **STUBBORN**, AND WOULD NOT COOPERATE WITH US. SO WE KILLED ANOTHER AS A LESSON...

WH- WHAT... ?!

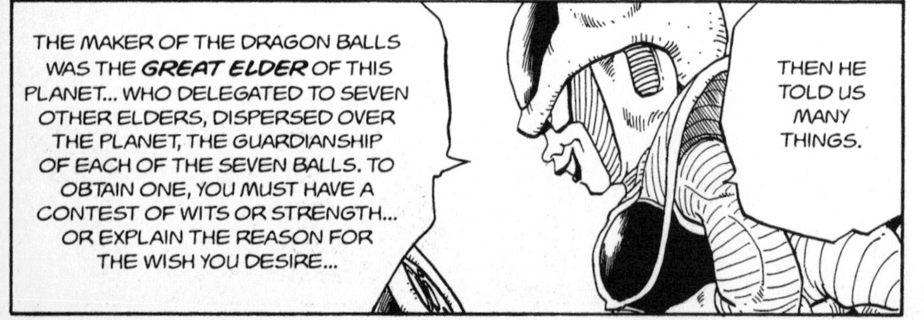
THEN HE TOLD US MANY THINGS.
THE MAKER OF THE DRAGON BALLS WAS THE **GREAT ELDER** OF THIS PLANET... WHO DELEGATED TO SEVEN OTHER ELDERS, DISPERSED OVER THE PLANET, THE GUARDIANSHIP OF EACH OF THE SEVEN BALLS. TO OBTAIN ONE, YOU MUST HAVE A CONTEST OF WITS OR STRENGTH... OR EXPLAIN THE REASON FOR THE WISH YOU DESIRE...

HOW COULD YOU...?
HOW...

THE OTHER THREE WE OBTAINED EASILY. EVERYONE WAS HAPPY TO OBLIGE.

SO THAT'S HOW IT IS...
I SEE...

AND ONLY AFTER YOU ARE DEEMED WORTHY BY EACH OF THE SEVEN ELDERS CAN YOU POSSESS THEM ALL.
I TRIED TO DO AS HE SAID, BUT HE SAID HE WOULD NEVER GIVE THE BALL TO ME...
SO I KILLED HIM. WHICH MADE IT QUITE TROUBLESOME LOCATING THE FIRST BALL.

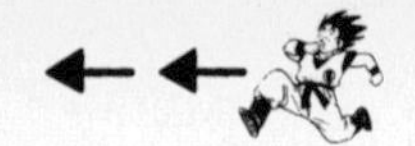

"HAPPY TO...!" ***LIAR*** !!
YOU KILLED THEM TOO!
THE OTHER ELDERS WOULD ***NEVER*** GIVE THE DRAGON BALLS TO ***YOU***!

NO, REALLY. THEY OBLIGED QUICKLY WHEN WE DID THIS.

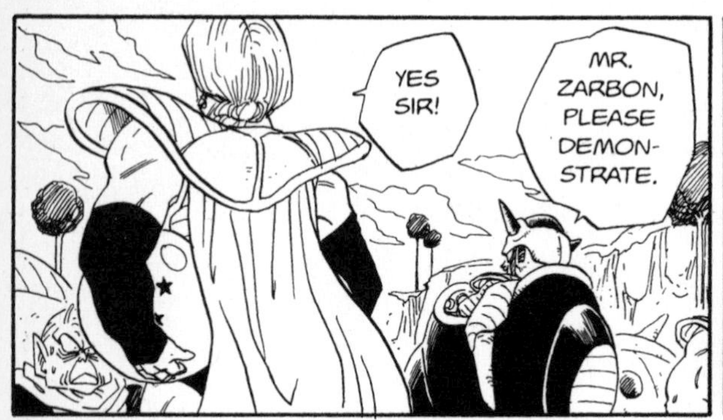
MR. ZARBON, PLEASE DEMON-STRATE.
YES SIR!

TMP

KRAK

WHAT--
!!!!
DOMP

SHP
DON'T !!!

!!
MONSTER !!!!

!!

HWA
GACK !!!!

BWOOM

...GA...

TMP

fap

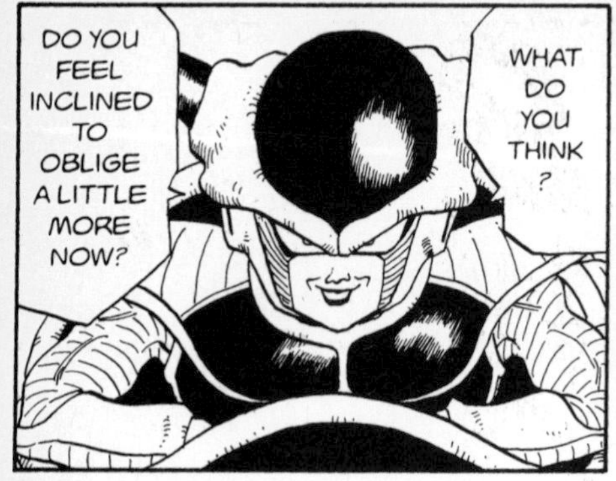
DO YOU FEEL INCLINED TO OBLIGE A LITTLE MORE NOW?
WHAT DO YOU THINK ?

H-HOW AWFUL.
I...I CAN'T BELIEVE THEM...

WH...WHY DO YOU WANT THE DRAGON BALLS...? WHAT WILL YOU WISH FOR?
...
OH, A SIMPLE WISH. MERELY ETERNAL LIFE FOR MYSELF.

COULD IT BE...?
MAYBE... THEY'RE NOT IN ON IT WITH VEGETA...

TH-THEN WHAT ABOUT VEGETA...? H-HE WAS ALSO AFTER ETERNAL LIFE...
WH- WHAT... ?!

TO A CREATURE LIKE YOU... EVEN IF IT MEANS MY LIFE...
I CANNOT GIVE THE DRAGON BALLS

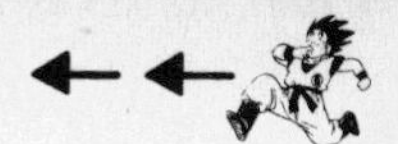

HO HO. SO YOU WOULD CHOOSE DEATH...
RATHER THAN MAKE ME HAPPY...

PEOPLE ON THIS PLANET REALLY ARE STUBBORN. BUT WOULD YOU BE ABLE TO REMAIN SO STUBBORN...WHEN FACED WITH THE DEATHS OF THOSE CHILDREN?

WH- WHAT ?!
SURELY NOT EVEN ***YOU***... WOULD MURDER CHILDREN...!!

UNH... !

...!!

pi
pi
pi

COMBAT POWER... ?!
MASTER FREEZA! LOOK!!

HWOOOO

OH... ?!

AH !!!

NEXT: The Reinforcements!

TITLE PAGE GALLERY

DRAGON BALL
ドラゴンボール
EARTH IS SAVED, FOR NOW...BUT THIS IS JUST THE CALM BEFORE THE STORM!
DBZ:48 • The Bittersweet End
TORIYAMA 鳥山明 AKIRA
BIRD STUDIO

Here are the chapter title pages which were used when **Dragon Ball Z Vol. 5** was originally published in Japan in **Shônen Jump** magazine. Some were previously published in Viz's **Dragon Ball Z** monthly comic series; some have never before been seen in America!

ドラゴンボール

DRAGON BALL

DBZ : 50 • Destination Namek

NEW ADVENTURES WAIT FOR US!!
kira Toriyama
鳥山明
BIRD STUDIO
ONWARD!!

DRAGON BALL

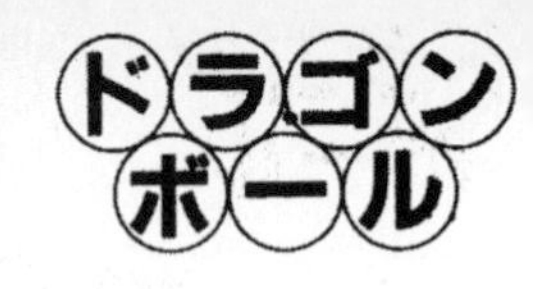
ドラゴンボール

WHAT HATH POPO WROUGHT?

DBZ:50 • The Mysterious Spaceship

Akira Toriyama

BIRD 鳥山明 STUDIO

DRAGON BALL

DBZ : 51 • 3...2...1...Lift Off!

DON'T MESS WITH ME IN OUTER SPACE !!!
BULMA
DRAGON BALL
CAPSULE CORP.
CAPSULE CORP.
CAPSULE CORP.
CAPSULE CORP.
Akira Toriyama
鳥山明
BIRD STUDIO

ドラゴンボール
DRAGON BALL
DBZ:52 • The Return of Vegeta
THE MOMENT THEY DREADED IS AT HAND!
Akira Toriyama
BIRD STUDIO

DBZ:54 The Mysterious Strangers

DRAGON BALL

PLANET NAMEK SPIRALS INTO CHAOS!!!

Akira Toriyama
鳥山明
BIRD STUDIO

DRAGON BALL

Akira Toriyama
鳥山明
BIRD STUDIO

DBZ:55 • Vegeta's True Power!

☆Who's Who on Planet Namek☆

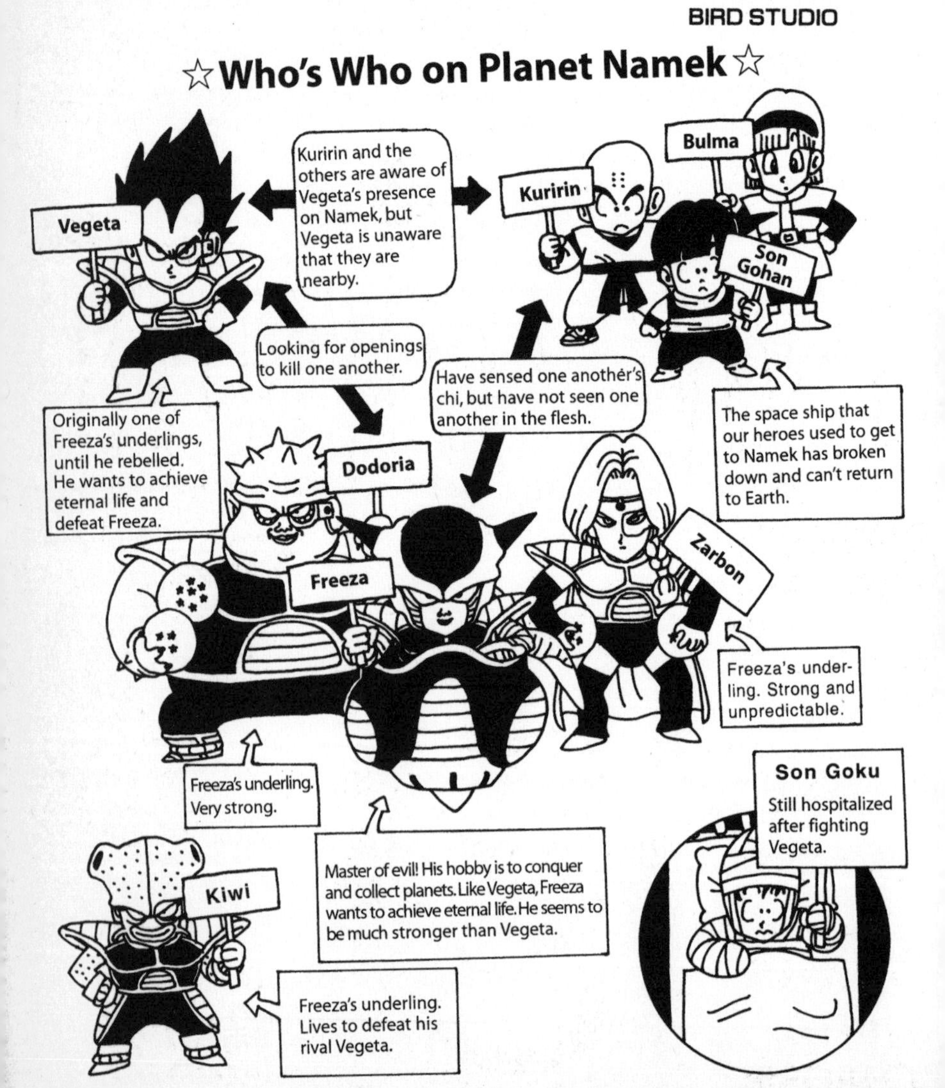
Kuririn and the others are aware of Vegeta's presence on Namek, but Vegeta is unaware that they are nearby.
Bulma
Kuririn
Vegeta
Son Gohan
Looking for openings to kill one another.
Have sensed one another's chi, but have not seen one another in the flesh.
Originally one of Freeza's underlings, until he rebelled. He wants to achieve eternal life and defeat Freeza.
The space ship that our heroes used to get to Namek has broken down and can't return to Earth.
Dodoria
Zarbon
Freeza
Freeza's underling. Strong and unpredictable.
Freeza's underling. Very strong.
Son Goku
Still hospitalized after fighting Vegeta.
Kiwi
Master of evil! His hobby is to conquer and collect planets. Like Vegeta, Freeza wants to achieve eternal life. He seems to be much stronger than Vegeta.
Freeza's underling. Lives to defeat his rival Vegeta.

DRAGON BALL

YO!!! DID YOU MISS ME?

DBZ:56 • Goku Returns! Again!

Akira Toriyama
鳥山明 BIRD STUDIO

DRAGON BALL

EVERYONE'S WAITING!! NOW IT'S TIME TO GO!!!

Akira Toriyama
鳥山明
BIRD STUDIO

DBZ : 57 • Son Goku's Spaceship

APSULE
CORP.
亀

DRAGON BALL

I'LL BECOME STRONGER STILL!

ドラゴンボール

Akira Toriyama
鳥山明
BIRD STUDIO

DRAGON BALL
307
KAME
CAPSULE
BS893

DRAGON BALL

story and art by Akira Toriyama

The journey begins when Bulma, teenage genius, meets Goku, a naive young monkey-tailed boy who has never left his mountain home. But Bulma needs Goku's help...and his super-strength...on her quest to find the seven magic Dragon Balls which, when gathered, will grant any wish! Along the road, they meet strange friends and stranger foes in this weird, wild, funny adventure.

BEFORE HE WAS THE WORLD'S STRONGEST HERO HE WAS THE WORLD'S STRONGEST BOY!

CALL OR GO ONLINE FOR DRAGON BALL MONTHLY COMICS!

Order by phone at **(800) 394-3042**

Fax **(415) 348-8936**

Online **www.vizkids.com**

GRAPHIC NOVELS

192 pages

$14.95 each

Vol.	Catalog No.
1	C-T-DB001
2	C-T-DB002
3	C-T-DB003
4	C-T-DB004
5	C-T-DB005
	(May '01)

Dragon Ball ©1984 by BIRD STUDIO.
All rights reserved.
First published in Japan in 1984 by SHUEISHA, Inc., Tokyo.

VIZ COMICS

www.vizkids.com

MOBILE SUIT GUNDAM WING

EPISODE ZERO

8•Issue Comic Series

On Sale Now From VIZ COMICS

©SOTSU AGENCY • SUNRISE
©HAJIME YATATE • YOSHIYUKI TOMINO • KATSUYUKI SUMISAWA • AKIRA KANBE
First published in Japan by Gakken Co., Ltd.

S0-AUY-920

THE ART OF
MOBILE SUIT GUNDAM WING

A collection of killer art from the most popular show on the Cartoon Network!

MOBILE SUIT GUNDAM WING
BLIND TARGET

ON SALE NOW!

MARCH 2001

VIZ COMICS™

VIZ www.viz.com
ANIMERICA www.animerica-mag.com
j-pop.com www.j-pop.com

©Sunrise/Sotsu Agency
©Hajime Yatate/Yoshiyuki Tomino/Sakura Asagi/Akemi Omode
First published in Japan by Gakken Co., Ltd.